T0256902

Accelerating Cloud Adoption

Optimizing the Enterprise for Speed and Agility

Michael Kavis

Beijing · Boston · Farnham · Sebastopol · Tokyo

Accelerating Cloud Adoption

by Michael Kavis

Published by O'Reilly Media, Inc., 1005 Gravenstein Highway North, Sebastopol, CA 95472.

O'Reilly books may be purchased for educational, business, or sales promotional use. Online editions are also available for most titles (*http://oreilly.com*). For more information, contact our corporate/institutional sales department: 800-998-9938 or *corporate@oreilly.com*.

Acquisitions Editor: Jennifer Pollock	**Indexer:** nSight, Inc.
Development Editor: Sarah Grey	**Interior Designer:** Monica Kamsvaag
Production Editor: Caitlin Ghegan	**Cover Designer:** Randy Comer
Copyeditor: Sonia Saruba	**Illustrator:** Kate Dullea
Proofreader: nSight, Inc.	

December 2020:   First Edition

Revision History for the First Edition

2020-11-25:   First Release

See *http://oreilly.com/catalog/errata.csp?isbn=9781492055952* for release details.

978-1-492-05595-2

[LSI]

Contents

Foreword

I am privileged to be able to write the foreword to Mike Kavis' second book. In early 2014, while leading the global cloud transformation for a multinational financial services firm, I personally purchased two dozen copies of Mike's previous book, *Architecting the Cloud: Design Decisions for Cloud Computing Service Models*. I freely handed out copies to the members of the CIO Council that governed all technology programs at the bank. I also gave copies to all of the managing directors who reported to me in the Office of the CTO, and to senior leaders in the technology organizations supporting the corporate, consumer, and capital markets businesses. This was the first time most of these leaders were introduced to concepts such as infrastructure as a service (IaaS) and platform as a service (PaaS). I advised my colleagues to read just the first seven chapters, particularly Chapter 3: Cloud Computing Worst Practices. The goal of that recommendation was to make everyone aware of what not to do, before we embarked on a journey to architect and enable a global private cloud with IaaS and PaaS service models. Enthusiasm for the new-new thing often has to be mitigated by an up-front recognition that there are always complex risk trade-offs associated with any technology transformation, and some words of wisdom by Mike Kavis, who had gone down the path before, was advice to be well considered.

In this book I see the same wisdom and caution offered for how cloud operating models are the essential element to figure out and get right before embarking on a public cloud or a multicloud journey. I have spoken many times to customers and in various public forums about the concepts of cloud economics, cloud speed, cloud scale, and cloud safety & security. These are all key architectural and operational objectives for any cloud, whether private, hybrid, public, edge, or multicloud. The goal is to accurately quantify the economic trade-offs of capex and opex, enable faster speed of delivery of infrastructure and applications, and have the ability to scale up/down and/or scale out/in dynamically, while all the time ensuring that resiliency, safety, and soundness are preserved through end-to-end security, resiliency, and disaster recovery policies and mechanisms. What is common to all of these goals is achieving maturity in cloud operating models, and the people, processes, and technologies that all have to come together to achieve a level of operational maturity to enable the desired business outcomes.

The analogy Mike makes with the evolution of power utilities in the early part of the 20th century is apropos for the type of technology transformation to utility-like consumption models for infrastructure and software services. However, moving electrons around is actually much simpler than moving complicated application workloads and their data to a cloud consumption-based operating model from a traditional enterprise IT cost-managed operating model. And the reality for most customers is that it is not an all-or-nothing proposition, but some combination of a private, hybrid, public, and colocation cloud model based on a complicated set of application and business risk-management constraints, as well as the economics, speed, scale, reliability, and security trade-offs mentioned above.

Cloud computing models offer significant opportunities for businesses to enable new types of services, delivered at a velocity and scale previously unimagined. The key enabler is all the software, much of it originating in the open source community, that is able to deliver very high degrees of automation, both by the cloud providers in delivering their services and by the cloud consumers delivering applications built on those services. There is, however, an element of risk concentration that must be given due consideration. Just as electrical power utilities can incur planned or unplanned outages affecting millions of users, risk concentration of applications and services in public cloud utilities can incur outages since they usually offer only 99.9% reliability of the infrastructure. You have to bring your resiliency models along with your applications when you make the journey to the cloud. No application is an island unto itself and usually has an ecosystem of services that provide the essential life-support mechanisms that application teams have come to rely on. Many application developers do not fully understand resiliency the way that outage-hardened IT infrastructure people do, so they have to work together as a joint team, which may not be a natural tendency. The later chapters of this book dig into the operational models that enable you to ensure that operational resiliency and recoverability are part of the cloud strategy, planning, and operating model. Site reliability engineering models are a key part of the process to achieve high degrees of resiliency in a cloud world. Just as I did when recommending Mike's first book to my former colleagues, I strongly recommend you read to at least Chapter 7: Cloud Operations and Reliability, so that you understand the failure models and what you can do to avoid them.

—Greg Lavender, Ph.D.
SVP & CTO VMware, Inc.
Palo Alto, CA

Preface

The purpose of this book is to help enterprise leaders develop plans to accelerate cloud adoption in their organizations. Adopting cloud computing is a transformation for most organizations. You can't just plug your old processes directly into the cloud and expect to succeed; everyone in your enterprise, inside and outside IT, will need to adopt a new mindset. As a leader, you will spend a lot of time explaining why change is necessary. You'll need to create a clear vision of what "good" looks like that others can follow.

Leaders must not focus entirely on the technology aspects of cloud computing without giving equal time and effort to the organizational changes and process-oriented design required to deliver software in the cloud. Too often, technology leaders shrug off the need to redesign operating models and business processes, labeling these steps as the "soft stuff." Ignoring the "soft stuff," though, will slow your adoption and can make it extremely challenging, if not impossible, to achieve the ROI you expect from moving to the cloud.

While there is information in this book that will be useful to all, the book is geared toward the needs and challenges of large enterprises and the people who lead them, from IT team leaders to the C-suite. It's meant to help you make decisions, design your operating model, rethink your technological culture, and get buy-in for your cloud adoption from even the most hesitant corners of the organization. It is first and foremost about cloud strategy. While I discuss numerous technical topics, I do so only at a conceptual level; you won't find code or step-by-step instructions here. For those seeking a deeper dive into the technical details, I recommend sources throughout the book. My goal here is to help you think through how cloud fits into the big picture of the long-term strategy of your enterprise.

How to Use This Book

The first four chapters of this book, Part I, highlight why cloud adoption requires rethinking our organizational structures and implementing new ways of working and thinking about the entire software development life cycle. There are numerous comparisons and real-life examples of how radically different building and operating in the cloud is from on-premises physical infrastructure. The emphasis here is on *why* these changes are so crucial to successful cloud adoption. Chapter 2 through Chapter 4 are conveniently titled "Technology," "People," and "Processes," for the three key focus areas of any successful journey to the cloud.

If you feel that you already know the differences and understand *why* organizations need to change, feel free to head straight to Chapter 5, where I discuss operating model design. From there, Part II of the book discusses the question of *what* exactly needs to change and *how*.

If you do skip the first four chapters, keep the book handy for future reference. You will meet resistance on your cloud journey, because not everybody understands the value of the cloud and why the changes you are pushing for are so necessary. Part I is designed to help you make your case for cloud-based changes not only in technology but in human resources (including training and recruiting) and in processes. I have also prepared some slides to help you communicate the concepts discussed in this book in your presentations.

O'Reilly Online Learning

For more than 40 years, O'Reilly Media (*http://www.oreilly.com*) has provided technology and business training, knowledge, and insight to help companies succeed.

Our unique network of experts and innovators share their knowledge and expertise through books, articles, and our online learning platform. O'Reilly's online learning platform gives you on-demand access to live training courses, in-depth learning paths, interactive coding environments, and a vast collection of text and video from O'Reilly and 200+ other publishers. For more information, visit *http://oreilly.com*.

How to Contact Us

Please address comments and questions concerning this book to the publisher:

O'Reilly Media, Inc.
1005 Gravenstein Highway North
Sebastopol, CA 95472
800-998-9938 (in the United States or Canada)
707-829-0515 (international or local)
707-829-0104 (fax)

We have a web page for this book, where we list errata, examples, and any additional information. You can access this page at *https://oreil.ly/accelerating-cloud-adoption*.

Email *bookquestions@oreilly.com* to comment or ask technical questions about this book.

For news and information about our books and courses, visit *http://oreilly.com*.

Find us on Facebook: *http://facebook.com/oreilly*

Follow us on Twitter: *http://twitter.com/oreillymedia*

Watch us on YouTube: *http://www.youtube.com/oreillymedia*

Acknowledgments

This book is dedicated to all of the people I have worked with and learned from during my cloud journey, which started in 2007.

I would like to thank my wife, Eleni, for allowing me to prioritize work over play one more time, mostly between 10 p.m. and 2 a.m. A very special thank you to my editor, Sarah Grey, who took all of my random thoughts, brain dumps, and long-winded sentences and turned them into a book that flows well and gets my points across clearer than I could have articulated on my own. Rock star! Thanks also to my technical reviewers: Greg Lavender, Ken Corless, Dave Linthicum, and Jeff Armstrong. Their keen eyes made this a better book; any errors are mine.

PART | I

Introduction:
The Shift to the Cloud

Thomas Edison, as we all know, is credited not only for inventing the light bulb but for commoditizing electricity. Many other scientists also contributed, both before and after Edison, but it was Edison's assistant, Samuel Insull, who built a business model that would commoditize electricity and make it available as a service. Insull came up with the concept of the power grid, which enabled economies of scale that made electricity available to factories and other businesses as a utility.[1] Today, we pay for electricity based on consumption: the more you use, the more you pay; the less you use, the less you pay. If this sounds like your cloud experience, read on.

Before electricity was a public utility, companies had to create and manage their own electricity, with waterwheel mills or hydraulic generators located close to their assets that needed power. These were incredibly expensive, closed systems. Only the richest could produce enough power to run product assembly lines, warehouses, offices, and sweatshops. The operating model was very simple back then. Such firms usually employed a VP of Electricity, who managed a staff of skilled electricians and generator operators. This group owned the power, and all other parts of the company were consumers of that power and at the mercy of permissions from the power provider.

The introduction of the power grid changed all this. Now any company of any size could access the same power grid at the same cost, without the overhead of purchasing and managing their own power generators. This was a game

---

1 In the book *The Big Switch* (W. W. Norton), Nick Carr introduces us to the famous analogy of adoption of the power grid. Here I extend Carr's thesis to show how the challenges of embracing the new ways of working that came with power are analogous to those of embracing cloud computing.

changer. Now, power (computing) was available for more purposes and was used for multiple applications, not just for a single purpose. Corporations could now automate assembly lines, appliances, and numerous other electrical devices at a fraction of the cost.

New inventions spawned everywhere, disrupting industries and paving the way for new business models and products. While investors and business owners embraced these innovations, workers were not always as excited—after all, when was the last time you hired a milkman, used an ice delivery service for refrigeration, or saw a lamplighter at dusk? Electricity displaced these workers. Nor were the VPs of Electricity and their domain experts all that excited to see electricity become available simply by plugging a cord into an outlet in the wall. What was going to happen to their jobs?

It is easy for us today to look at the invention of the power grid as a no-brainer. Of *course*, companies would quickly adopt and embrace power as a utility instead of maintaining their own power departments and equipment. But the shift to the grid did not happen overnight. Large companies had made big investments in legacy technologies; they needed time and money to transition to the new model. Of course, VPs of Electricity fought tooth and nail against the new model—how could they give up control of something so critical to a third party? Over time, it no longer made sense to build and maintain generators. Companies migrated from the old do-it-yourself (DIY) electricity model to the pay-as-you-go electricity model, and their operating models changed to reflect new business processes.[2]

Even once everyone was on board, migration was a long, hard road. Many companies focused their efforts entirely on technical aspects. But the legacy method of owning and operating electricity came with years of best practices—and corresponding processes that enforced those best practices. The old operating model put the electricity department at the center of the universe: all other departments had to go through it to request power, and brought their old processes and operating model with them to the new era of electricity. Even though power consumers could now access power instantly, they were still forced to go through the electric department for permission, fill out the same forms, attend the same review meetings, and satisfy the same checklists—because "that's how we do it here." So even though power was widely available, it still took a long

---

2 Institute for Energy Research, "History of Electricity" (*https://www.instituteforenergyresearch.org/history-electricity*).

time for power consumers to get the access they needed. This approach made it hard for companies to realize the benefits and business advantages that the power grid should have brought them.

If any of this sounds like a cloud transformation that you have been a part of or have heard about, there's good reason for that. A century later, as we move from running on physical infrastructure to consuming infrastructure as a service, many cloud transformations are stalling for similar reasons. Too many companies focus their cloud adoption strategy solely on the technology, with little to no consideration for redesigning their legacy operating models and business processes. They, too, find it difficult to realize the advantages of cloud as a utility.

That's why I wrote this book: I want your cloud adoption journey to be different. I'll show you how to calibrate not only your tech but your people and your business processes to take maximum advantage of the cloud and move past outdated ways of doing things, so your cloud transformation can begin creating value for you much faster, and with fewer roadblocks.

Specialization and Silos of Knowledge

The shift from private power generation to the grid has a lot in common with the shift from the mainframe computing of the 1960s and 1970s to today's cloud computing. For several decades, mainframes were the sole source of computing infrastructure for most companies. With the birth of minicomputers, servers, and personal computers, however, work could be distributed on smaller machines at a fraction of the cost. New skills and domain expertise were required to manage all the new hardware and new operating systems. Networks and storage devices became the norm. Organizations experimented with different, more horizontal operating models to contain the sprawl of technology. They sought to manage the risks of change by adding review boards and gates, centers of excellence, and other processes. The mainframe teams were no longer the center of the universe; no longer did all standards, permissions, and change management go through them. Each technology domain now had its own standards, access controls, and change-control processes.

One result of this change in IT system complexity was that domain knowledge became walled off into "silos" of specialization. Each team was measured on its own goals and objectives, which often conflicted with those of the other groups that consumed or supplied services to that group. Each team thus built processes around inputs (requests for service) and outputs (delivery of service) to its organization, in the hope of having more control over achieving its goals and objectives. For example, the security team would create request forms, review processes and best practices to which other departments would have to adhere; if there was a problem, the security team could point to its process as proof of its due diligence. The governance team had its own processes, as did the change management team, the project management team, the quality assurance team, the operations team, and so on.

This model served its purpose well when software was built as large, monolithic applications that were deployed on physical infrastructure and planned in quarterly or biannual release cycles. As inefficient as it was for a development team to navigate through all of the mostly manual processes across the numerous silos, release cycles were long enough to allow for these inefficiencies.

Today, however, speed to market is more of a competitive advantage than ever; customers expect new features and fixes much more frequently than before. Companies that stay mired in the ways of the past risk becoming the next Blockbuster Video, their popularity vanishing into obscurity as the world moves on without them. The 2019 State of DevOps Report (*https://services.google.com/fh/files/misc/state-of-devops-2019.pdf*) concluded that top-performing teams that employed modern DevOps best practices deployed 208 times more frequently, had lead times 106 times from commit to deploy, resolved incidents 2,604 times faster, and had a rate of change failure 7 times lower than teams that did not embrace DevOps.

Cloud computing can enable the agility that so many companies seek, but cloud technology by itself is not enough. To keep up and to create value from that agility, companies must move away from the "VP of Electricity" model of doing business and transform to new ways of working.

Today's chief information officers (CIOs) have an extremely tough job: they have to balance "keeping the lights on" (that is, keeping the money flowing) with improving agility and quality, and investing in new technologies. Pick up any trade magazine and you will see success stories of large companies adopting emerging technologies such as cloud computing, machine learning, artificial intelligence, blockchain, DevOps, Scaled Agile Framework (SAFe), and site reliability engineering (SRE). Each new trend is designed to solve a specific set of problems, but it takes a combination of tools, trends, methodologies, and best practices to deliver cloud computing at scale.

Even as CIOs embrace cloud computing and adopt many of these new technologies and methodologies, they must work within the policies set forth by their governance, risk and compliance (GRC) team and their chief information security officer (CISO), neither of which are known for welcoming change in most companies. The GRC and CISO have a strong incentive to make sure the company never ends up on the front page of the *Wall Street Journal* for a breach or system failure. At the same time, the CIO is asked to deliver more value faster. These are competing priorities, and to fulfill them, many organizations are shifting traditionally domain-specific functions like testing, security, and operations to software engineering teams and even business units.

The challenge this presents is that many engineers are not sufficiently skilled to take on these new roles effectively. It only takes one incident—say, a server with an open port to the web—to cause a CISO to lock everything down, to the point where nobody can get timely work done in the cloud. When domain expertise shifts without the company rethinking existing organizational structures, roles, responsibilities, and processes, the end result is usually undesirable—and sometimes even catastrophic.

Patterns and Antipatterns in Cloud Adoption

To embrace the cloud and create the capabilities to build and run software in it at scale, IT leaders need to step back and redesign their organizations around the cloud. We must rethink the entire software-development value stream, from ideation to ongoing production.

No two cloud transformations are the same, but the patterns for success and the antipatterns of failure are very common. Companies that succeed in the cloud do so after many tough lessons. Nobody gets it right at the beginning. But if you start your transformation expecting some bumps and bruises along the way, you can get off the sidelines and start making progress. Your culture must embrace transparency and continuous learning, and you should expect to adjust and improve constantly.

At tech conferences like AWS re:Invent, Google Cloud Next, or DevOps Enterprise Summit, you'll hear plenty of success stories. Those who haven't achieved that level of success can get disheartened because it can seem like all the other companies are getting it right. Don't be fooled: most success stories represent a product line or business unit within a very large organization, not the entire organization. Other parts of their organization may still be in the very early stages. Keep your chin up. This book will share lessons about what to do and, more importantly, what *not* to do as you embark on your cloud journey.

What's more important than getting it right at the beginning? Actually *starting*. Too many organizations get so caught up in trying to create the perfect low-risk strategy, changing CIOs and consulting partners constantly, that they never actually begin doing the work. They have nothing more than years of strategy documents and PowerPoint decks to show for their efforts, while their competitors keep advancing across the cloud maturity curve.

Organizations that get stuck at this stage tend to see the cloud not as a transformation, but as a technology project. Some companies are so conservative that they put too many restrictions on moving forward with any significant effort in the cloud. This might be more of a failure than moving to the cloud and running into problems with availability and resiliency. At least with the latter, you're gaining experience and increasing your maturity.

When companies don't recognize the need to transform themselves and to build, operate, and think about software differently, they take their old business processes, tooling, and operating model with them to the cloud—which almost always results in failure.

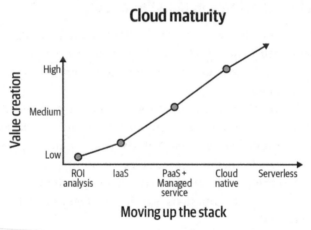

Figure 1-1. The cloud maturity curve. Where does your organization sit?

I've been consulting on cloud adoption since 2013, and I've seen just about every customer request you can imagine, from companies at all levels of cloud maturity. To capture this variation, I created the maturity curve in Figure 1-1. What this image shows is that when most organizations start their cloud journey, they focus on the ROI of moving to the cloud. At this point early in their journey, they think of the cloud in the same context as the datacenter: they're thinking about servers instead of services. The value they can get from this mindset is low in comparison to the value that can be achieved in the cloud. After gaining experience building and running applications in the cloud, they start to move up the stack and leverage platform as a service (PaaS) solutions or fully managed services from the cloud providers, like database as a service. This allows them to achieve better speed to market and more operational efficiencies. As they continue to move up the stack and start embracing cloud native and serverless architecture concepts, they start creating business value at high speed. At this level of maturity, the full promise of cloud can be realized. The problem is, very few get past the ROI analysis and infrastructure as a service (IaaS) mindset to come close to achieving the desired ROI.

When I first started, most of my clients requested either an overall cloud strategy or wanted my analysis of either total cost of ownership (TCO) or return on investment (ROI) for a cloud initiative. At the time, convincing their CEOs and boards that cloud computing was the way forward was a hard sell for IT leaders. About 80% of the requests were focusing on private cloud, while only 20% were for the public cloud, almost exclusively Amazon Web Services (AWS). In November 2013, at its annual re:Invent conference, AWS announced a wide variety of new enterprise-grade security features. Almost immediately, my phone began ringing off the hook with clients looking for advice on public cloud implementations. A year later, those clients' work requests had completely flipped, with over 80% for public cloud and 20% for private cloud.

As public cloud adoption increased, companies moved to the cloud or built new workloads in the cloud much faster than they had traditionally deployed software. Two common antipatterns emerged.

THE WILD WEST

Developers, business units, and product teams now had access to on-demand infrastructure, and they leveraged it to get their products out the door faster than ever. They had no guidelines or best practices, and development teams took on responsibilities they'd never had before. Rather than developing a systematic approach and implementing it across the organization, though, many companies simply left cloud decisions to individual parts of the organization: a lawless, "Wild West" approach.

Here is a tale of two companies. Alpha Enterprises (as I'll call it) had five business units (BUs), each with its own development and operations teams. The centralized IT team had always provided infrastructure services to the BUs, which were extremely dissatisfied with IT's long lead times and lackluster customer service. The BUs looked at cloud computing as an opportunity to divorce themselves from IT and speed up their delivery times. They all had early successes deploying their first application or two in the cloud. But as they added more applications, they were woefully unprepared to support them. Customers started experiencing lower levels of reliability than they were accustomed to.

Then, one day, the dangerous Heartbleed bug was discovered.[3] The security and operating-system teams scrambled to patch impacted systems across the organization—but they had no visibility into the exposure of the cloud-based systems the BUs had built. It took several weeks for the security team to access and fully patch the vulnerability in those systems. Months later, security performed an assessment and found two more systems that had never been patched.

BetaCorp, on the other hand, had a central IT team that built and managed all of its approved operating systems. The BUs leveraged a standard build process that pulled the latest approved operating system from the central team's repository. When the bug was discovered, the central team updated its operating-system images and published the new version. The BUs simply redeployed their applications, which picked up the latest patched version of the operating system, and the vulnerability was eliminated that same day across all of BetaCorp's cloud applications.

Part of the problem at Alpha Enterprises, and companies like it, is that each BU is "reinventing the wheel": researching, buying, and implementing its favorite third-party tools for logging, monitoring, and security. They each take a different approach to designing and securing the environment. More than a few also implement their own continuous integration/continuous delivery (CI/CD) toolchains with very different processes, resulting in a patchwork of tools, vendors, and workflows throughout the organization.

This has both positive and negative consequences. Companies like Alpha Enterprises deliver value to their customers faster than ever before—but often expose themselves to more security and governance risks than before, as well as deliver less resilient products. This lack of rigor and governance makes production environments unpredictable and unmanageable.

---

3 Synopsys describes Heartbleed (*https://heartbleed.com*) as a bug that "allows anyone on the internet to read the memory of the systems protected by the vulnerable versions of the OpenSSL software. This compromises the secret keys used to identify the service providers and to encrypt the traffic, the names and passwords of the users, and the actual content. This allows attackers to eavesdrop on communications, steal data directly from the services and users, and to impersonate services and users."

COMMAND AND CONTROL

The opposite of the freewheeling "Wild West" antipattern was a military-style, top-down, command-and-control approach. In these companies, groups that were highly motivated to keep things in line—such as management, infrastructure, security, and GRC teams—put the brakes on public cloud access. They built heavily locked-down cloud services and processes that made developing software in the cloud cumbersome. These processes were often decades old, designed during the period when deployments occurred two or three times a year and all infrastructure consisted of physical machines owned by a separate team.

Let's look at another example. A well-established healthcare company I'll call Medical Matters acquired an up-and-coming startup, CloudClaims. CloudClaims had created a cloud-based claims processing application that automated the age-old paper claims processes that were still standard in the industry. Instead of taking weeks, CloudClaims provided same-day claims completion. When Medical Matters' security and risk teams assessed the new technology their company had acquired, they were appalled to find out that the same team that built the code was deploying it into production. They took that responsibility away from the CloudClaims staff and mandated that they follow the standard, proven process that had been in place for two decades at Medical Matters.

Suddenly, the deployment rate dropped from three times a day to once a month. What used to be a fully automated process now had to be broken into steps to allow for architecture and security review meetings, a biweekly change-control board meeting, and email approvals from two levels of executives. The CloudClaims developers challenged these processes, even showing the executives why their process was less risky than the process that they were being forced to use. Medical Matters would not budge. Eventually, key CloudClaims team members left Medical Matters. The product itself started to lose its value, because it could no longer respond to the market demand at the rate it once had.

Medical Matters' approach destroys one of the key value propositions of the cloud: agility. I have seen companies where it took six months to provision a virtual machine in the cloud—something that should take five minutes—because the command-and-control cops forced cloud developers to go through the same ticketing and approval processes required in the datacenter.

This approach created very little value even as companies spent huge sums on strategy and policy work, building internal platforms that did not meet developers' needs. Worse yet, this approach created an insurgent "shadow IT," as it did at Alpha Enterprises: groups or teams began running their own mini-IT organizations to get things done because their needs were not being met through official channels.

These antipatterns have raised awareness of the need to focus on cloud operations and to invent a new cloud operating model. Since 2018, my clients have been clamoring for assistance in modernizing their operations and designing new operating models. Many are a few years into their journey.

At the start of the cloud adoption journey, enterprises focus a lot of attention on cloud infrastructure. They learn a lot in this phase, improving their technical skills for building software and guardrails in the cloud. They often start at the IaaS layer, because years of working with physical infrastructure have made them comfortable dealing with infrastructure. As the enterprise's cloud experience matures, they begin to realize that the true value of cloud is higher up in the stack. That's when they look into PaaS and software as a service (SaaS).

At the same time, development shops have been embracing high levels of automation and leveraging concepts like CI/CD. This book will show how concepts like DevOps, cloud-native architecture, infrastructure as code, and cloud computing have changed traditional operations.

The Datacenter Mindset Versus the Cloud Mindset

When you start building in the public cloud, you are basically starting from scratch: no existing cloud datacenter, no guardrails, no financial management tools and processes, no disaster recovery or business continuity plan, just a blank canvas. The conventional wisdom is to just use the tools, processes, and organizational structures you already have, from the datacenter, and apply them to the cloud. That's usually a recipe for disaster.

When applications are moved, refactored, or built new on the cloud, they are being deployed to a brand-new virtual environment that is radically different from the datacenter environments that people are used to. The processes and policies governing how work gets done in a datacenter have typically evolved over many years. Along with these legacy processes comes a whole host of tools that were never intended to support software that runs in the cloud. If these tools are not cloud native, or at least "cloud friendly," getting them to work effectively (or at all) in the cloud can involve a painful integration period. This creates friction for getting software out the door. It can also create unnecessary complexity, which can increase costs, reduce performance, and even reduce resiliency. All of this makes it challenging—and sometimes impossible—to automate software build-and-release processes from end to end.

Some of the questions IT teams need to ask when designing a cloud strategy include:

- What should we do when incidents, events, or outages arise?
- What processes should we follow to deploy software?
- What's the technology stack for the products we're building and managing?
- What processes should we follow to introduce new technology?

Let's look at a few examples. In the command-and-control antipattern, one common desire is to keep existing on-premises logging solutions in place instead of moving to a cloud-native solution. If you do this, all logs must be sent from the public cloud back to the datacenter through a private channel. You'll incur data transfer costs and create an unnecessary dependency on the datacenter. What's more, these legacy logging solutions often have dependencies on other software solutions and processes, which in turn create unnecessary (and sometimes unknown) dependencies between the cloud and the datacenter that can cause cloud outages.

Here is another example. My team conducted an assessment of a client's tools. We recommended tools that would work well in the cloud and advised them on which existing tools should be replaced by a more cloud-suitable solution. One tool we recommended replacing dealt with monitoring incoming network traffic. The group that managed the tool dug in and refused: they were comfortable with the old tool and didn't want to have to manage two tools. This created a single point of failure for all of the applications and services running in that company's public cloud. One day the tool failed—and so did all of that company's cloud applications.

The lesson here is that clinging too closely to tools that are not well suited for the cloud will hamper your cloud adoption efforts and lead to avoidable errors and outages. Instead of sticking to what's comfortable, work to reduce the number of datacenter dependencies, and have a plan to mitigate any failures.

As companies rethink their approach to the cloud, a new operating model that brings domain experts closer together can reduce these incidents.

Enterprises that have been building and running datacenters for many years often have a challenge shifting their mindset from procuring, installing, maintaining, and operating physical infrastructure (the "VP of Electricity" mindset) to a cloud mindset, where infrastructure is consumed as a service. Table 1-1 shows some of the mindset changes required to leverage the cloud. To be real, the items on the right for the cloud native approach are not things you get on day one of your cloud journey. They represent what you should strive for and work toward adopting over time. But if your team is stuck in the datacenter design mindset, you will lose a lot of the value of the cloud.

Table 1-1. The legacy datacenter mindset versus the cloud-native mindset

Legacy datacenter approach	Cloud-native approach
Procure new infrastructure	Pay for consumption
Rack and stack infrastructure	Run automated scripts
Patch servers	Destroy and redeploy in CI/CD pipeline
Service requests for infrastructure	Enable self-service provisioning
Scale vertically	Scale horizontally
Plan for hardware refresh every 3-5 years	Does not apply
Multiple physical disaster recovery sites	Real-time disaster recovery across zones and regions
Networking appliances	Networking APIs
Multiple approvals and review gates	Push-button deployments

SHARED RESPONSIBILITY

When you buy a house, you are making an investment in a plot of land and in any physical structures on that land. You are responsible for all maintenance, landscaping, cleaning, snow removal, and everything else that comes with home ownership. When you rent a house, however, you are paying for the *time* in which you inhabit the rental property. It is the landlord's responsibility to maintain the property. The biggest difference is between renting and buying is what you, as the occupant of the house, have control over.

When you leverage the cloud, you are renting time in the cloud provider's "house." What you have control over is very different from what you control in your own datacenter. For people who have spent their careers defining, designing, and implementing processes and technologies for the controls they are responsible for, shifting some of that control to a third party can be every bit as challenging as handing over responsibility for a home you've lovingly restored and renovated.

The two groups that probably struggle the most to grasp the shared responsibility of the cloud are auditors and GRC teams. These teams have a set of processes and controls in place for physically auditing datacenters. They expect to be able to apply these exact processes and controls in the cloud. The problem is, they can't. Why? Because these datacenters belong to the cloud service provider (CSP), such as Amazon or Google, which has a duty to make sure your data is safe from its other clients' data. Would you want your competitor walking on the raised floor at Google where your software is running? Of course not.

With the shared responsibility model, shown in Figure 1-2, the CSP is responsible for logging and auditing the infrastructure layer, not the client. An acquaintance at a CSP once came to me about a client who was adamant about getting all of the CSP's logs. The client wanted to ingest the logs into their company's central logging solution. The client was so used to being required to store this type of information for audits that they simply would not budge. I finally had to explain that in the new shared responsibility model, that data would no longer be available to them. They would have to educate their audit team and adjust their processes.

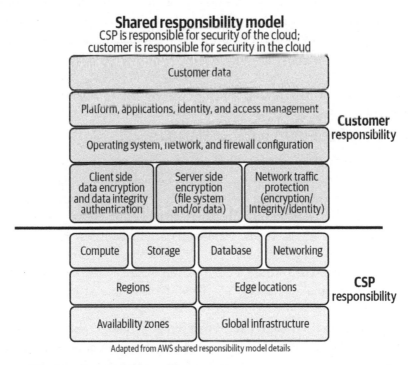

Figure 1-2. The shared responsibility model

To be clear, the policy that required the client to store those logs was still valid. What had completely changed was how to satisfy that policy in the cloud. If auditors and GRC teams cannot change their mindset and accept new ways of satisfying their policy requirements, their companies might as well not go to the public cloud. But should auditors or GRC teams really hold an entire company back from leveraging cloud computing?

In the datacenter world, teams traditionally organize around skill domains related to infrastructure: storage, network, servers, operating systems, security, and so forth. In the cloud, much of this infrastructure is abstracted and available to the developers as an API call. In the datacenter mindset, if you need storage, you create a ticket asking another team to perform a variety of tasks to stand up physical infrastructure, like a storage area network (SAN). In the public cloud, though, developers have access to storage as a service and can simply write code to "provision" the necessary storage.

To build a secure, compliant, and resilient network, datacenters have networking teams which leverage third-party vendors for appliances, routers, gateways, and other tools. In the cloud, most of the features that these tools provide are available as a service. For functionality where the cloud providers don't provide the necessary network security, third-party solutions are available as SaaS or as a pay-as-you-go model, and can be procured either directly from the vendor or through the CSP's marketplace. There are usually no physical assets being purchased. Gone are the days of buying software and paying a quarter of the purchase price for annual maintenance. In the cloud, you pay for what you use.

USE WHAT YOU NEED, NOT JUST WHAT YOU HAVE

Before cloud computing, almost all of the development I was involved in was deployed within datacenters that my company owned. For each piece of the technology stack, a specialist in that technology took responsibility. A team of database administrators (DBAs) installed and managed database software from vendors like Oracle, Microsoft, and Netezza. For middleware, system administrators installed and managed software like IBM's Websphere, Oracle's WebLogic, and Apache Tomcat. The security team took responsibility for various third-party software solutions and appliances. The network team owned physical and software solutions.

Thus, whenever developers wanted to leverage a different solution from what was offered in the standard stack, it took a significant amount of justification. The solution had to be purchased up front, the appropriate hardware procured and implemented, contractual terms agreed upon with the vendor, annual maintenance fees budgeted for, and employees and/or consultants trained or hired to implement and manage the new stack component.

Adopting new stack components in the cloud can be accomplished much more quickly, especially when these stack components are native to the CSP—*if* you don't let legacy thinking and processes constrain you. For example:

- No long procurement process is necessary if a solution is available from the CSP as a service.

- No hardware purchase and implementation is necessary if the service is managed by the CSP.

- No additional contract terms should be required if the proper master agreement is set up with the CSP.

- There are no annual maintenance fees for each service thanks to the pay-as-you-go model. The underlying technology is abstracted and managed by the CSP, so new skills are only needed at the software level (for example, learning how to consume the API).

Let's say that Acme Retail, a fictitious big-box retailer, has standardized on Oracle for all of its online transaction processing (OLTP) database needs and Teradata for its data warehouse and NoSQL needs. A new business requirement comes along that requires a document store database in the next four months.

In the old model, adopting document store databases would require new hardware, software licensing, disk storage, and many other stack components. Acme employees would have to get all of the relevant hardware and software approved, procured, implemented, and secured, at significant effort and expense. In addition, Acme would need to hire or train DBAs to manage the database technology.

Now let's look at how much simpler this can be in the public cloud. Acme is an AWS shop, and AWS offers a managed service for a document store database. Most of the steps mentioned above are totally eliminated. Acme no longer needs to worry about hardware, software licensing, additional DBAs to manage the database service, or new disk storage devices—in fact, it doesn't need any procurement services at all. All Acme needs is to learn how to use the API for the document store database, and it can start building its solution.

Let's say that Acme hires a consulting team to deliver the new feature. The consultants recommend purchasing MongoDB as the preferred document store database to satisfy the requirements to store and query documents. Acme has no prior experience with MongoDB, which means it will have to go through the procurement process. However, within Acme's current set of processes, there is no way to get approvals, procure all of the hardware and software, train or hire DBAs, and implement the database in just four months. Therefore, Acme decides to leverage its existing Oracle database, a relational database engine, to solve the problem. This is suboptimal because relational databases are not a great solution for storing and retrieving documents. Document store databases were built specifically for that use case. But at least Acme can meet its deadline by leveraging existing database technology.

This decision process repeats itself over and over from project to project: Acme keeps settling for suboptimal solutions due to the constraints of its legacy processes. The technical debt just keeps mounting.

Now let's see how different this can all be if Acme decides to embrace a database-as-a-service solution in the public cloud.

After doing some testing in a sandbox environment in the cloud, the consultants determined that the document store managed service on our favorite CSP's platform is perfect for Acme's requirements. They can start building the solution right away because the database is already available in a pay-as-you-go model, complete with autoscaling.

Leveraging stack components as a service can reduce a project's timeline by months. It allows you to embrace new technologies with a lot less risk. Perhaps most importantly, you no longer have to make technology compromises because of the legacy challenges of adopting new stack components.

Consuming stack components of a service provider provides greater flexibility for architects. It is important for all IT domains to understand this. If they don't, there is a good chance that they'll end up forcing legacy constraints on their cloud architects and wind up building suboptimal greenfield solutions in the cloud that create new technical debt.

DevOps

One of the key messages of this book is that you cannot achieve success in the cloud by focusing only on cloud technology. To succeed at scale in the cloud, enterprises must make changes not only to the technology, but to the organization structures and the legacy processes that are used to deliver and operate software. Embracing DevOps is a key ingredient to successfully transforming the organization as it adopts cloud computing. But what is DevOps, really?

One of the biggest misperceptions about the term *DevOps* is that it is a set of technologies and tools that developers and operators use to automate "all the things." DevOps is much more than tools and technologies, and it takes more than just developers and operators to successfully embrace DevOps in any enterprise. Many people will shrug off this debate as nothing more than semantics, but understanding DevOps is critical for any organizational strategy. If you see DevOps as no more than automating CI/CD pipelines, you will likely leave out many important steps required to deliver in the cloud at scale.

There are many ways to define DevOps. Back in 2014 I defined it (*https:// www.astroarch.com/tvp_strategy/devops-engineer-25120*) as "a culture shift or a movement that encourages great communication and collaboration (aka teamwork) to foster building better-quality software more quickly with more reliability." I went on to add that "DevOps is the progression of the software development lifecycle (SDLC) from Waterfall to Agile to Lean and focuses on removing waste from the SDLC."

But don't take my word for it; look at the work of the leading DevOps authors, thought leaders, and evangelists. Gene Kim, coauthor of popular DevOps books such as *The Phoenix Project, DevOps Handbook,* and *The Unicorn Project* (all IT Revolution Press), defines it as:

> *The set of cultural norms and technology practices that enable the fast flow of planned work into operations while preserving world class reliability, operation and security.*
>
> *DevOps is not about what you do, but what your outcomes are. So many things that we associate with DevOps fits underneath this very broad umbrella of beliefs and practices . . . of course, communication and culture are part of them.[4]*

Buntel and Stroud, in their book *The IT Manager's Guide to DevOps* (XebiaLabs), define DevOps as "a set of cultural philosophies, processes, practices, and tools that radically removes waste from your software production process."[5] Similarly, *The DevOps Handbook* asks us to "imagine a world where the product owners, Development, QA, IT Operations, and Infosec work together, not only to help each other, but also to ensure that the overall organization succeeds."

---

4 Gene Kim, keynote presentation at the DevOps Enterprise Summit, San Francisco, November 2017, quoted in Mike Kavis, "The Four Stages of DevOps Maturity" (*https://www.forbes.com/sites/mikekavis/ 2017/11/17/the-four-stages-of-devops-maturity/#72efabce2f62*).

The popular and influential book *Accelerate, the Science of Lean Software and DevOps*, by Forsgren, Humble, and Kim (IT Revolution Press), describe DevOps as:

> *The new ways, methods, and paradigms . . . to develop software, with a focus on Agile and Lean processes that extended downstream from development and prioritized a culture of trust and information flow, with small cross-functional teams creating software.*

As you read through these definitions, you'll notice lots of references to goals: in particular, quality, trust, sharing and collaboration, and removing waste. Let's discuss each one.

Quality

As we strive to improve speed to market, we must not sacrifice quality along the way. The users of our products and services expect those products and services to work. The more things don't function as expected, the lower overall customer satisfaction will be. In addition, quality issues lead to unplanned work, which can lead to long hours, high pressure to fix critical issues quickly, lower productivity, and burnout. DevOps aims to ensure high levels of quality throughout the entire SDLC to create better products and services, and happy customers and workers.

Trust

Silo structures breed a lack of trust between the silos, which typically have conflicting priorities. For example, the security team focuses on reducing threats, the testing team on finding defects, the operations team on stability, and the development team on speed to market. Each silo builds processes for interacting with the other silos with the goal of improving the likelihood of meeting the year's objectives. So the security team adds request forms, review meetings, and standards, seeking visibility into potential risks in the software and infrastructure being introduced to the system. The problem is that, often, the security team does not consider the other team's goals and objectives. The same holds true for the other silos. Meanwhile, development builds processes to expedite building and deploying software to production. This directly conflicts with the testing team's goal of catching defects before the code is released to production, and creates challenges for operations, whose goal is to maintain acceptable levels of reliability, because they can't effectively track the changes and the potential impacts to dependent systems.

Narrow-minded goal setting within silos creates mistrust and organizational conflict between teams. DevOps aims to create more trust throughout the SDLC, so groups can better collaborate and optimize their processes, resulting in higher agility and morale.

Sharing and collaboration

Sharing and collaboration go hand in hand. When experts in different domains work closely together, they produce better outcomes. A key component of collaboration is to share information: goals, lessons learned, feedback, and code samples. Without good collaboration, projects tend to fall into a waterfall mentality. For example, one development team I worked with finished coding and testing and requested a review from the security team—which rejected their unit of work because it didn't meet their security requirements. Fixing these issues took several rounds of back-and-forth—and then they had to repeat the process for operations, compliance, and architecture. This led to longer lead times from when a customer requested a feature to when that feature was usable in production. The result was that business users became frustrated with the long lead times and started looking for IT solutions outside of IT.

DevOps aims to foster better collaboration across different technology domains like these, so it can address issues early. It also aims to create a culture of collaboration, where everyone works toward common outcomes.

Removing waste

Much of the DevOps mindset was adopted from Lean manufacturing processes and from writings like Eliyahu Goldratt's *The Goal* (North River Press), which focuses on optimizing the production assembly line by identifying and removing waste and process bottlenecks. The processes for building and deploying software are often riddled with huge amounts of manual intervention, review gates, multiple approvals, and numerous other bottlenecks that reduce agility and often contribute very little to their goals of eliminating risks and improving quality. DevOps aims to drive system thinking throughout the SDLC with the goal of streamlining work and creating a culture of continuous improvement.

If DevOps embraces all of these ideas, why do so many organizations create a new silo called DevOps and focus on writing automation scripts, without collaborating with the product owners and developers? Some companies take their existing operations teams, adopt a few new tools, and call that DevOps. While these steps are in themselves progress, a nonholistic approach to DevOps will not deliver its promise. "DevOps" silos often lead to even more waste, because the focus is usually exclusively on the tools and scripting, not on the real goals of the product teams they support.

Tip

What about DevSecOps? NoOps? AutoOps? AIOps? Aren't those things all better than DevOps? Should I be adopting those instead?

To most mature DevOps practitioners, DevOps is *all* of the things I just listed. When you concentrate on outcomes, you use the techniques that best help you deliver those outcomes. These new terms emphasize what their creators see as underrepresented aspects of the system (security, automation, AI, etc.). They help consultants and their clients feel current. But make no mistake: there is little true difference between these next-generation buzzwords and the old-fashioned (circa 2009) term *DevOps*.

Follow the principles in this chapter. Then call it whatever you want.

To understand DevOps, it is critical that we understand its roots. Its evolution started back in 2008. At the Agile 2008 Toronto conference, as he recalls it (*https://www.youtube.com/watch?v=Y_u84PNrX9g*), Agile developer Andrew Shafer gave a presentation entitled "Agile Infrastructure." Belgian infrastructure expert Patrick Debois was the only attendee. The two discussed how to use Agile infrastructure to resolve the bottlenecks and conflicts between development and operations, and their conversation blossomed into a collaboration. They created the Agile Systems Administration Group to try to improve life in IT.

At the 2009 O'Reilly Velocity Conference, John Allspaw and Paul Hammond got the IT community (including Debois) buzzing with their presentation "10+ Deploys Per Day: Dev and Ops Cooperation at Flickr" (*https://www.youtube.com/watch?v=LdOe18KhtT4*). Back then, deploying multiple times a day was almost unheard of and would have been widely considered reckless and irresponsible. Inspired by the presentation, Debois set up a conference and invited his network on Twitter. He named it DevOpsDays and used the hashtag #DevOps when promoting it on Twitter. Were it not for Twitter's 140-character limit at the time, we would likely have had a less succinct movement in the industry.

It is easy to see why many people think that DevOps is just about developers and operators working together. However, the DevOps net has since been cast much more broadly. Today DevOps touches all areas of business. Many start their DevOps journey looking only at automating the infrastructure or the application build process, but high-performing companies with more maturity in DevOps are redesigning their entire organizations and processes, both inside and outside of IT.

Companies that enjoy success in their DevOps journey tend to share some common beliefs. These include:

- Changing the company culture and mindset is a critical success factor.

- Removing waste and bottlenecks from the SDLC helps drive business value.

- Shifting from reactive to proactive operations improves reliability.

- It's important to start somewhere and then continuously learn and improve.

- DevOps and the cloud require a new operating model and organizational change.

Enterprises that embrace change and continuous learning look very different three or four years years into their journey. Table 1-2 shows the typical order in which companies address bottlenecks to improve delivery and business outcomes. Usually, as they make strides removing one bottleneck (for example, inconsistent environments), they then progress to resolve their next big bottleneck (for example, security).

Table 1-2. Bottlenecks and pain points

Step	Bottleneck/pain point	Solution
1	Nonrepeatable, error-prone build process	Continuous integration (CI)
2	Slow and inconsistent environment provisioning	Continuous delivery (CD)
3	Inefficient testing processes and handoffs	Shift testing left/test automation
4	Resistance from security team; process bottlenecks	Shift security left, DevSecOps

Step	Bottleneck/pain point	Solution
5	Painful handoff to operations teams, forced to use legacy tools/processes, poor MTTR	Shift ops left, new operating models (platform teams, SRE, etc.)
6	Slow service-level agreements from tiers 1–3 support	Shift support left, new operating models
7	Slow and painful approval processes for governance, risk, and compliance	Shift GRC left, stand up cloud GRC body

These are just some of the problems I see, and the corresponding changes implemented to remove the bottlenecks. Many enterprises have large initiatives to reskill their workforce and even rethink the future of work. The incentives we offer workers must change to achieve the desired outcomes; procurement processes must change as we shift from licensing and maintenance to pay-as-you-go models; in short, every part of the organization is affected in one way or another.

Conclusion: People, Processes, Technology

Today we can build and deploy software faster than ever before. Cloud computing is a big reason why. CSPs are providing developers with a robust service catalog that abstracts the underlying infrastructure, allowing developers to focus more on business requirements and features. When cloud computing first became popular in the mid- to late 2000s, most people used the *infrastructure as a service* (IaaS) mindset. As developers became more experienced, they started leveraging higher levels of abstraction. *Platform as a service* (PaaS) abstracts away both the infrastructure and the application stack (the operating system, databases, middleware, and so forth). *Software as a service* (SaaS) vendors provide full-fledged software solutions; enterprises only need to make configuration changes to meet their requirements and manage user access.

Each one of these three cloud service models (IaaS, PaaS, and SaaS) can be huge accelerators for a business which no longer has to wait for the IT department to procure and install all of the underlying infrastructure, application stack, and build and maintain the entire solution.

In addition, technologies like serverless computing, containers, and fully managed services (such as databases as a service, blockchain as a service, and streaming as a service) are providing capabilities for developers to build systems much faster. I will discuss each of these concepts in more detail in Chapter 2. I'll also look at immutable infrastructure and microservices, two important concepts that accelerate speed to market in the cloud.

But this transformation is bigger than CI/CD pipelines or Terraform templates. You learned in this chapter that organizational change, culture change, thinking and acting differently, modernizing how work gets done, and leveraging new tools and technologies are at the heart and soul of DevOps.

To scale DevOps across an organization, a new operating model is required. It's a little ironic: IT departments have introduced so many new technologies, yet those IT departments themselves largely just kept running with the same old processes and structures, despite major changes in the underpinning technology. Even fairly large advances in methods in IT, most notably Agile, only changed processes in *parts* of silos, rather than looking holistically at the entire IT organization. Adopting these concepts in a silo without addressing their impact on people, processes, and technology across the entire SDLC is a recipe for failure. (Chapter 5 will discuss some of the patterns and antipatterns for operating models.)

Gaining that holistic view requires paying close attention not only to technology, but to the processes that run the tech and the people who carry out those processes. In the next three chapters, I'll look at each of these in turn.

2

Technology

My first tech job out of college was working as a consultant writing code for a steel company in the south. The technology stack was rather simple back then. We had three generations of mainframes: Burroughs, DEC PDP-11/70, and the brand-new IBM 3090. We wrote in COBOL, Fortran, and Assembler. There were three options for storing data: tape, Db2, and IMS databases. The operating model was simple, too. A small group of people managed the mainframe, the software, and the databases, and the rest of us wrote code.

When an app broke, the person who wrote the code was paged and had to fix it. It was very common that there was one developer per program. This was long before the days of service-oriented architectures, microservices, and even the internet. Running an IT shop was much easier back then because there were fewer technologies to manage, the infrastructure was centrally managed, and almost everyone was writing code in the same languages.

A simplified operating model in my mainframe days looked like Figure 2-1. The mainframe team managed the full stack of the mainframe, which included the infrastructure, the programming languages (such as COBOL, Fortran, and RPG), and the database technologies (IMS, Db2, and so forth).

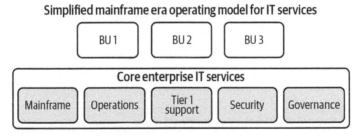

Figure 2-1. Simplified operating model during the mainframe era, circa 1980s

They also provided tape service, managed the execution of the jobs, and were the review and approval gates for any changes to the environment.

Then the internet, Windows, Linux, and three-tier web architectures became popular. The previous operating model could no longer support the new demands on IT. In addition to the mainframe, we now had PCs distributed all over the company, and our datacenters became filled with minicomputers, robotic tape backup devices, storage devices, and complex networking infrastructure. This led to much more complex operating models like the one depicted in Figure 2-2.

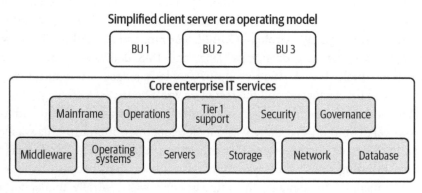

Figure 2-2. A more complex operating model during the client server era, circa 1990s

In the mainframe era, the mainframe group managed the full stack. In the client server era, technology was broken out into multiple stack components that had the flexibility to be leveraged in ways specific to the application requirements. You had to tailor the application to the available infrastructure.

When client-server architectures arrived, you could tailor the infrastructure to the application requirements. Not only could architects now request specific infrastructure to meet their needs, they also had more choices for database technologies. This prompted many enterprise IT departments to create a silo of database experts to deliver database technologies to the business unit. But it didn't stop with databases. There were more choices for operating systems, programming languages, storage and network technologies, and so forth. The operating model had changed from having a mainframe team own all compute, network, storage, and database technologies, to domain experts delivering all of these services independently.

Now architects had more choices to optimize hardware, middleware, and database technologies for their application requirements, but the complexity of managing the underlying technologies increased substantially. Many new processes emerged from each technology domain, so navigating core IT processes became challenging and riddled with waste. Along the way, domain experts became so immersed in delivering their part of the technology stack, that IT services started becoming less knowledgeable about the applications for which they were providing services.

As technology advanced over the next few decades, our operating models changed (see Figure 2-3), but not quite so drastically. Very few companies actually redesigned their operating model, instead just adding more services to their existing model. Navigating IT became so challenging that many BUs started looking to external vendors to meet their needs.

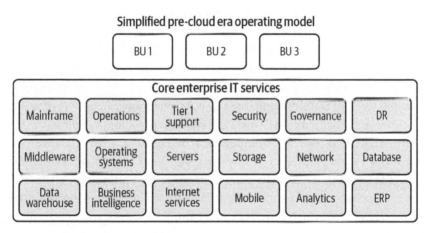

Figure 2-3. Pre-cloud operating model, circa 2000s

As we move to the cloud, these old operating models are insufficient for building and deploying software in the future. You can't plug cloud into your existing operating model and expect great results. We as an industry need to rethink our approach to delivering services to our customers. We need a new operating model that's optimized for the cloud.

But before we build that, let's take a step back to fully understand the fundamental differences between cloud computing and traditional computing on-premises with physical infrastructure.

I'll look at a few technological changes that hold particular significance for the cloud transition: infrastructure as code (IaC), CI/CD, immutable infrastructure, microservices, and containers.

Infrastructure as Code (IaC)

In the cloud, we provision infrastructure with a set of APIs. Whether we are working with private clouds in our datacenter or public clouds with our favorite CSP, the underlying physical infrastructure is abstracted from us. We simply write code to spin up instances of virtual machines. This is obviously a drastic change from how we provision infrastructure in the physical datacenter.

Infrastructure skills in the cloud require programming skills. We no longer "rack and stack" physical servers and other hardware components. Instead, we write short snippets of code that are executed to automatically provision virtual infrastructure for things like servers, networks, storage devices, and much more.

Since we can do this in code, do we need infrastructure people to do it? The answer depends on how your organization chooses to govern the provisioning process. A common approach is to have cloud infrastructure people create the standard *blueprints* or *images,* as they are often called. The developers are often allowed to leverage these blueprints in a self-service capacity to spin up new infrastructure as they need it. To do this effectively, we must rethink our roles, responsibilities, and business processes in order to optimize the flow of work.

For example, the traditional process flow for requesting and deploying infrastructure might look like the one depicted in Figure 2-4 (which assumes the hardware procurement process is already completed) and could take anywhere from days to months. This is the classic Information Technology Infrastructure Library (ITIL) change-management workflow. Typically, there is a process owner for each process box, which requires one or more meetings and approvals to get to the next step.

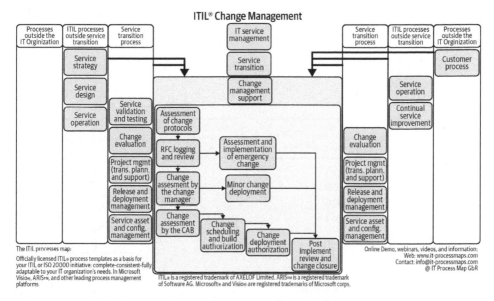

Figure 2-4. Traditional process flow for requesting and deploying infrastructure

A flow optimized for cloud might look more like Figure 2-5 (which does not require a hardware procurement process), and the elapsed time could be minutes if the processes are optimized. In this flow, almost the entire process is fully automated. It meets all of the requirements of the ITIL process, without all of the meetings and reviews. It accomplishes this by automatically scanning the code to ensure the proper coding standards and best practices are in place, the security policies are accounted for, the infrastructure is properly tagged for asset manage-ment and billing, and so forth. Everything that previously required meetings and approvals can now be enforced. If the code does not meet the enforcement poli-cies, the build fails and the developer must fix the issues before proceeding any further. This allows the system to auto-approve each step along the way and elim-inate numerous meetings.

The cloud infrastructure is automatically created, leveraging approved blue-prints that already have patched operating systems, and supporting monitoring, logging, and security-tool agents installed so that operations can monitor it. Again, numerous meetings and setup tasks are eliminated via automation.

Obviously the flow in Figure 2-5 is simplified, but the point here is that much of the time required to deliver software in the old model can be fully automated in the new model while actually reducing risks of post-production incidents.

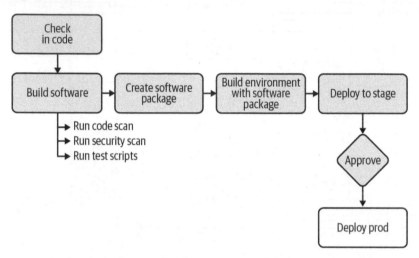

Figure 2-5. A cloud-optimized process flow for requesting and deploying infrastructure

You would think that comparing the two flows would be enough to get companies leaping into the cloud and thus drastically improving provisioning times. But in many cases, even when a company moves to the cloud, the provisioning time remains unchanged. Why? Because it only focused on the technology—not on the people and processes that make the technology work.

Let me offer you a cautionary tale. I once worked with a large provider of security software—I'll call it Mothership—that purchased a small, nimble security software startup, LittleFish. Prior to being acquired, LittleFish had brought new features to the market daily. Its platform team was made up of engineers with server, network, storage, and security skillsets who created scripts (infrastructure as code) that provided preapproved images of the necessary software stack components. The whole process took a day or two.

After the acquisition, the LittleFish team was required to follow Mothership's legacy process for requesting infrastructure. Suddenly, the same process was taking them up to six months—that's right, six *months*! Why? Because Mothership's process was a relic from a period when all infrastructure was physical and managed within the four walls of the datacenter. It included numerous steps and handoffs between teams that specialized in specific components of the technology stack: the server team, storage team, network team, security team, datacenter operations team, and on and on. Even though the engineers had the efficient scripts they'd created, they were still forced to go through the old process because their audit required gates and checklists, which were put in place "to protect the company."

Mothership had acquired a cloud-based company, but didn't reevaluate its operating model to leverage the cloud. The LittleFish cloud experts' ability to deliver ground to a halt, so the acquiring company couldn't extract the value it had expected out of the startup purchase. But, hey, at least the auditors were happy.

The reality is that we will always have to manage both cloud and noncloud infrastructure. Mainframe systems are still with us and will be for many more years. Not all workloads make sense to deliver in the cloud, and moving to the cloud is often a multiyear effort.

The mistake many companies make is that they want the SDLC processes for cloud to follow the familiar patterns they are used to from legacy processes. Those legacy processes, however, were not designed for developers running pre-approved infrastructure scripts in self-service mode. The engineers who wrote them couldn't have imagined that security policies and compliance controls would be built into a cloud platform in a pay-as-you-go consumption model. Nor did they expect infrastructure people's roles to be product-centric, like cloud service providers are.

I said it in Chapter 1 and I'll say it again: before moving to the cloud, take a step back and rethink your operating model. If you don't, your cloud journey is not going to deliver the ROI you envision.

Remember, one key component of getting a return on your cloud investment is your ability to *shut off the physical servers once you move an application to the cloud*. The quicker you can accelerate cloud adoption, the sooner you can retire the physical infrastructure in the datacenter. Also, the sooner your organization becomes skilled at building net-new applications in the cloud, the sooner you can avoid building additional infrastructure in the datacenter for net-new applications. When we approach cloud computing with our old operating models and business processes, it often takes so much time and effort to get an application or service into production that the organization starts spending for infrastructure in both the datacenter *and* the cloud. If you don't improve time to market, you don't save money: in fact, you increase costs.

The result is usually a huge disparity between the ROI promised in the business plan and the actual ROI achieved, if any. When that happens, people pay the price with their jobs. Worse, some of these companies bring in new leaders and repeat the cycle two or three times with new scapegoats. Only when leaders address organizational and process challenges do they start to see mass adoption and reap the true benefits of the cloud.

CI/CD

Continuous integration and continuous delivery (CI/CD) are widely adopted methods of automating the software build and deployment process. CI is about building the code; CD is about delivering the infrastructure and deploying the build on it. CI/CD allows us to automate the software deployment process from end to end, with no human intervention. But, again, if you don't revisit your current state processes and organizational structures, that process will still be riddled with manual steps, review gates, multiple sign-offs, and other legacy constraints. We will discuss CI/CD in more detail when we discuss deployment processes in Chapter 4.

Immutable Infrastructure

Immutable infrastructure is a concept in which, once a compute instance (like a virtual machine or container) is deployed, it is never updated again. Instead, when it is no longer needed, it is replaced with a new compute instance that contains the necessary new software. (Informally, we also call it *destroy and redeploy* or *rehydrate*). Immutable infrastructure processes are different in several ways from the previous, mutable way of managing infrastructure.

When infrastructure is mutable, we apply updates directly onto that compute instance: that might be a security patch, a vendor update (like a new version of Tomcat), or a new version of the application server.

In 2011, cloud entrepreneur Randy Bias created an analogy about the difference in mindset between physical and cloud infrastructure that was so popular it's become a cliche in the field. He wrote:

In the old way of doing things, we treat our servers like pets, for example Bob the mail server. If Bob goes down, it's all hands on deck. The CEO can't get his email and it's the end of the world. In the new way, servers are numbered, like cattle in a herd. . . . When one server goes down, it's taken out back, shot, and replaced on the line.[1]

In the context of physical servers and virtual cloud servers, "pets" are "servers or server pairs that are treated as indispensable or unique systems that can never be down." They are, Bias explains, "manually built, managed, and 'hand fed.'" "Cattle," on the other hand, are:

Arrays of more than two servers, that are built using automated tools, and are designed for failure, where no one, two, or even three servers are irreplaceable. Typically, during failure events no human intervention is required as the array exhibits attributes of "routing around failures" by restarting failed servers or replicating data through strategies like triple replication or erasure coding. Examples include web server arrays, multi-master datastores such as Cassandra clusters, multiple racks of gear put together in clusters, and just about anything that is load-balanced and multi-master.

In the cloud, a best practice is to treat infrastructure as expendable (cattle). We use the term *immutable* to describe the processes of destroying and rebuilding a virtual machine (VM) in the cloud. In the legacy model, servers exist continuously, and a lot of time and effort goes into maintaining their health (Figure 2-6).

---

1 Randy Bias, "The History of Pets vs Cattle" (*http://cloudscaling.com/blog/cloud-computing/the-history-of-pets-vs-cattle*).

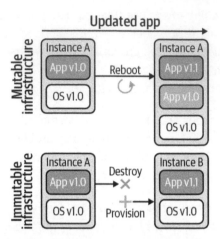

Figure 2-6. Updating with mutable versus immutable infrastructure (adapted from Josha Stella, Immutable Infrastructure (O'Reilly), fig. 1-1)

Release planning in the legacy model usually requires a backout or rollback strategy. Removing software updates from a production system can often create even more issues than what the unsuccessful release caused. Rollbacks can be extremely risky, especially in a complex system.

There are three major downsides to this approach. First, the software on the compute instance becomes more fragile over time, as more changes are made to the instance. Second, when updates have issues, backing out the changes can be complex and risky and may cause additional failures. Third, when you're working with a system at scale (hundreds or thousands of instances), it is extremely difficult to troubleshoot all instances and keep everything consistent. It would be much easier to just destroy and redeploy instances rather than tending to problem servers on an individual basis.

In the cloud, when a virtual machine is unhealthy, we can simply shut it down and create a new one. This allows us to focus our immediate attention on service-level agreements (SLAs) for availability, performance, reliability, and so on, instead of spending time trying to determine what caused the issue. Once the system is back to being stable and meeting its SLAs, we can then perform forensics on the data we captured from the terminated infrastructure. A best practice is to take a snapshot of the machine image, which you can use in conjunction with logging and monitoring tools to triage the problem.

Treating virtual machines in the cloud as immutable offers advantages for releasing software as well. Instead of designing complex rollback processes, we can implement a solution like the process shown in Figure 2-7.

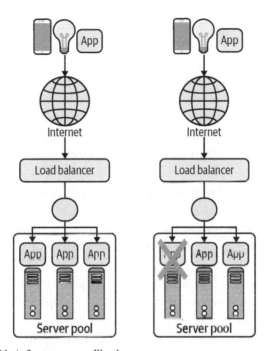

Figure 2-7. Immutable infrastructure rollback process

In this example, three web servers sit behind a load balancer. A *load balancer* receives network traffic and then distributes it across a number of servers. There are numerous techniques for distributing traffic, such as *round robin* (distributing traffic in a rotation), *least connection* (distributing traffic to the servers with the lowest total connections), and *source IP hash* (allows you to specify where the source IP should be directed).

You deploy the new software to three brand-new VMs and take a snapshot of the current VMs in case you need to roll back your changes. Then you attach the new VMs to the load balancer and start routing traffic to them. You can either take the older VMs out of rotation at this point or simply make sure no traffic gets routed to them. Once the new release looks stable, you can shut down the old VMs and detach them from the load balancer to complete the deployment. If there are any issues, you can simply reroute traffic to the older VMs and then shut down the new VMs. This allows you to stabilize the system without introducing the risk of backing out the software. Once the system is back to its stable state, you can focus on fixing the issues with the faulty deployment without worrying about impacting production.

This is just one of many ways to embrace immutable infrastructure for deployments. Companies with deep experience in this area can design advanced processes to create highly resilient systems, all of which can be fully automated.

The destroy-and-redeploy method also allows us to rethink how we support systems. Compare the processes for dealing with a faulty deployment with mutable and immutable infrastructure. With mutable infrastructure, when the compute instance is in an erroneous state due to issues with the deployment, the team must triage the compute instance in production and figure out how to return it to its previous clean state. With immutable infrastructure, the newly deployed instance is simply destroyed while the last good instance is simply redeployed in its place. This allows the operations team to quickly get the system back in a stable state without having to spend time trying to debug the system causing production issues. Once the system is back to running smoothly, the operations team can then start triaging the instance taken offline to figure out what was causing the issues.

The takeaway here is that when the way we perform a task changes (in this case, performing compute instance updates), the impact goes far beyond the technology. You'll need to look at the entire value stream to identify the effects on people (such as roles and responsibilities) and processes (such as incident management and event management) and adjust accordingly.

A *value stream* is the set of all steps in the SDLC, from the start of value creation until the delivery of the value to the customer. In the example above, the value stream is the entire process of updating the compute instance and the steps to back out changes if the update causes any issues. With mutable infrastructure, the value stream starts with the request for an update, all the meetings, checklists, approvals, and deployment processes required to deliver the value. The processes that support that value stream should look very different for immutable infrastructure, but unfortunately, the legacy processes often remain, adding waste to what should be a more efficient process. We will discuss value stream mapping, the process of analyzing value streams and optimizing them for speed and efficiency, in Chapter 4.

MICROSERVICES

Applications consist of many features. In the past, applications were delivered as a single process containing all of the functionality (referred to today as a monolith). The challenge with this approach was that each feature becomes dependent or tightly coupled to all of the other features of the application. Any change to any feature requires full testing and deployment of the entire application. This makes even the simplest changes to the application a risky proposition that requires the same oversight and governance as if a change was being made to the most critical features of the application.

Due to the tight coupling of features within monolithic applications, frequent deployments are seen as high risk and are discouraged. To improve speed to market, however, many architects have started looking at *microservices architectures* as a way to build loosely coupled systems that can be deployed as separate features called *services.*

In a microservices architecture, functionality is put into separate services that are independent from all other services. These services can be deployed independently and can also be scaled independently on its own infrastructure, as Figure 2-8 shows.

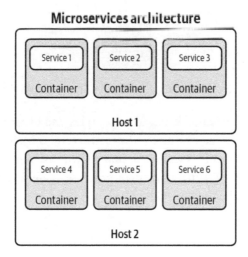

Figure 2-8. Microservices architecture

Each service runs in its own process and communicates with lightweight mechanisms, often an HTTP resource API.[2] Each service can be run on its own infrastructure, which can be a server, a virtual machine, or a container. This style of architecture is often referred to as *loosely coupled* because the services are independent of each other and not hardcoded to the underlying infrastructure.

The microservices approach radically changes how we build, deploy, and operate systems. Although the monolithic approach was slower and riskier, it was much easier to manage. Monoliths were typically deployed as a single process on mainframes, minicomputers, and as n-tier applications, such as a three-tier web architecture (Figure 2-9).

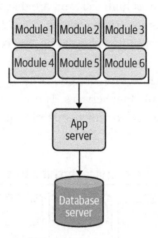

Figure 2-9. Infrastructure in the monolith

Microservices are usually deployed in complex and distributed infrastructure environments that leverage immutable infrastructure, containers, and favor environments that are elastic (scale up and down as needed), as shown in Figure 2-10. Each service runs as its own process, totally independent of all the other services that make up the product.

---

2 Martin Fowler goes into greater detail in "Are Microservices the Future?" (*https://martinfowler.com/articles/microservices.html*)

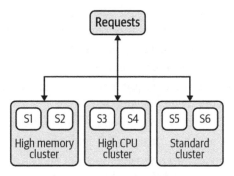

Figure 2-10. Scaling with microservices in a distributed infrastructure environment

The advantage of microservices is that each service can be deployed separately, resulting in much more frequent deployments. Developers can make small changes or add new services without being dependent on any other changes to the overall product. Companies that deploy multiple times a day typically have a microservices architecture or an architecture made up of many individual components, as Martin Fowler shows in Figure 2-11.

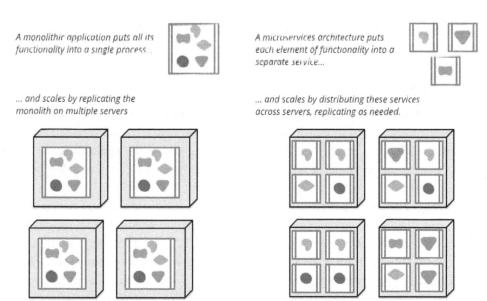

Figure 2-11. Microservices and monoliths. Image by Martin Fowler (https://martinfowler.com/articles/microservices.html), used with permission.

The disadvantage is that managing a system made up of many individual parts can be challenging. Traditional monolithic systems have a web frontend, a database, and backend processes, where most of the business logic is. In a microservices architecture, the system is made up of many independent services. Operations for a service-based product requires new tooling, new processes (especially for building and deploying software), and new skills.

The playbooks and tools we use to operate monolithic applications are not optimal for highly distributed, immutable, and elastic microservices architectures. In fact, microservices architectures can get so complex that they become almost unmanageable without high levels of automation and intelligent operations (see Chapter 7).

Building and operating microservices architectures requires greater levels of collaboration between development and operations; it favors cross-functional teams over technology-domain silos. Microservices architectures allow small changes to be built and deployed quickly and independently from the other features and services of the application. However, if you force microservices architectures to follow change and release management processes designed for monolithic applications, all of that agility goes out the door.

The bottom line here is that adopting microservices requires changes not only to the architectural approach, but also to the operating model and business processes.

CONTAINERS

Containers are, according to Google's definition (*https://oreil.ly/rcpk4*), "a logical packaging mechanism in which applications can be abstracted from the environment in which they actually run." This decoupling allows the application to run in almost any environment: a physical datacenter, a private cloud, any of the public cloud providers, even a laptop.

In my early development days in the late 1980s and early 1990s, I worked on AIX boxes that used logical partitions to create separate environments for different product teams to share space on large IBM AIX and RISC servers. In the early 2000s, much more innovation took place in the attempt to create more efficient methods of partitioning or isolation. The big breakthrough came in 2008 with the creation of the Linux Container project, which leveraged previous work from Google's cgroups, "which allow controlling and confining the amount of resources used for a process or for a group of processes."[3]

When PaaS solutions became popular in the late 2000s, they used containers to partition customers and to perform live updates and migrations on their platforms with zero downtime for their customers. But container technologies were relatively unknown to most developers until a company named dotCloud started working on an open source project called Docker in 2013.

I first heard about Docker back in January 2013, while I was writing my first book.[4] I went to the dotCloud office to interview CTO Solomon Hykes about PaaS. At the end of the interview we started sharing war stories about building startups, which I'd done in 2008. I said, "If I could do it all over again, I'd implement continuous delivery from the start." Solomon's ears perked up and he said he had something to show me, but he needed a couple more weeks to work on it. We agreed that the next time I was in San Francisco he would give me a demonstration.

A month later I met Solomon at the dotCloud office, where his team hosted their first demo day. There were five of us in the room. These demos became weekly events and the audience grew bigger every week. Solomon showed us what was soon to be named Docker, and our collective mouths dropped. For the first time ever, someone had made containers genuinely easy to use. Before Docker, you had to be a hardcore operating-system guru to work with containers. Now a developer could use a simple one-line "docker run" command (with some parameters) to build a running container with the desired software stack inside.

This was huge. Now I could create a standard environment that I could run anywhere—including my development machine, the test environment, and the production environment—in a container, isolated from the underlying infrastructure. I went home and wrote what might have been the first blog post about Docker, discussing how this could revolutionize the CI/CD process. But Solomon didn't stop there. Next up was using Docker containers to isolate microservices so that each one ran in an isolated environment, with no dependencies on any other microservice. This vision caught on fire, which created the need for a container orchestration engine to manage all that complexity. By 2015, Docker was

---

3 Irene Maida, "Containers: From the Origins to Docker" (*https://www.criticalcase.com/blog/containers-from-the-origins-to-docker.html*).

4 Michael Kavis, *Architecting the Cloud: Design Decisions for Cloud Computing Service Models* (Wiley).

valued at over a billion dollars, and many companies were changing the way they built and ran software.

By now, dotCloud had made Docker open source, sold its dotCloud assets, and pivoted to become a container company called Docker. It started building Docker Swarm, for container orchestration, and competed head-on with Mesos and Google's Kubernetes, which at the time of this writing in 2020 had become the de facto standard for container orchestration.

Before containers, systems engineers set up virtual machines and used tools like VMware's vSphere to manage them. Life was good. Then, all of a sudden, they had to manage clusters of containers using Docker, Kubernetes, and a host of new ecosystem tools to deal with container security, networks, storage, and more.

New uses for containers arose, too. Containers were originally built to run stateless services, but enterprises saw the opportunity to use them to lift and shift stateful legacy workloads to the cloud to minimize the amount of changes required to run software on the cloud.

Building and running container-based architectures successfully takes a serious shift in mindset. Containers are designed to be immutable. They usually run one service per container and have a much smaller footprint than their predecessor, the VM. Likewise, deploying, patching, monitoring, and auditing container-based architectures takes new skills, processes, and tooling.

Containers provide us with the opportunity to improve environment consistency, agility, scalability, portability, and isolation.

Their downside is their complexity. Managing hundreds or thousands of distributed clusters of immutable containers can be very challenging. Architectures like these require operators to know more about application architecture than ever before. Operators now need a mix of administrative and engineering skills. We are shifting from physical infrastructure to virtual infrastructure made of code, and that means revisiting and optimizing old processes and operating models to make them work in this new world.

Conclusion: New Tech, New Structure

This chapter discussed five key areas of recent major changes: IaaC, CI/CD pipelines, immutable infrastructure, microservices, and containers. Demand is increasing for many more new technologies, including analytics, machine learning, artificial intelligence, edge computing, augmented and virtual reality, and much more. Business leaders must figure out how to build new operating models that allow them to deal with the demands of the business while also absorbing all of the new technologies coming their way—*and* being more agile and cost effective. Restructuring how work gets done, as good leaders know, is all about the people doing that work. The next chapter reveals how successful companies are reengineering their approach to talent.

3

People

Technology is easy. People are hard. Adopting cloud computing requires significant change within an organization. Each process or technology change will affect real people and their lives. This chapter focuses on the skills your organization and its people will need for a successful cloud transition.

T-Shaped Teams

The previous chapter discussed technology changes like containers, microservices, and immutable infrastructure—all of which require new ways of working and new skills. That is a lot of change to throw at workers. You'll need people with a strong command of some of these concepts, and at least a basic understanding of all of them:

- Distributed computing
- How and when to use stateful versus stateless services
- Microservice architectures
- Container runtime and orchestration
- Serverless computing
- Building CI/CD pipelines
- Cloud security
- Hybrid and multicloud architectures

Companies are looking to hire *full stack engineers*, which refers to someone who is fluent in all of the skills I just listed. In my opinion, you have as much chance of spotting a unicorn as a full stack engineer. What we really should be aiming for is *full stack teams*, which are small teams made up of people whose *collective* expertise covers the full stack (see Figure 3-1).

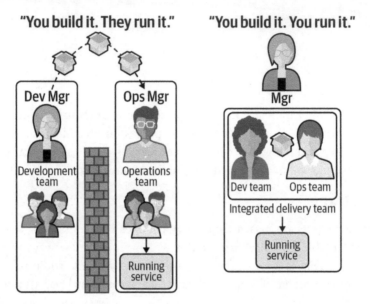

Figure 3-1. Full stack teams should be T-shaped

Traditional operating models tend to encourage workers whose knowledge is I-shaped, meaning that it goes very deep in a certain technology domain. In the cloud, we prefer to upskill our workers to be more T-shaped, meaning their expertise is deep in one or two areas but broad across the cloud spectrum. Full stack teams are made up of T-shaped workers, but there is a misperception that every *worker* has to be T-shaped: fluent in every part of the stack. That's not the case. Each worker should have broad knowledge and a solid understanding of cloud computing, but it is unreasonable to think that any worker could have deep expertise in all technology domains. Full stack teams are made up of people who have a breadth of knowledge in the stack, and a depth in a particular domain.

In some workplace cultures, transforming the workforce from I-shaped to T-shaped can be a shock to the system. Pulling this off requires a well-thought-out people strategy that includes investments in training programs and organization change management. Building T-shaped teams looks easy on a PowerPoint slide, but changing cultural norms is very hard. It requires an intentional approach that focuses on planning, training, communication, and coaching and requires strong leadership.

Many organizations are creating *cloud platform teams* that build and manage the approved, secured, and compliant cloud services from CSPs and vendors, and provide them to development teams, acting almost as an internal CSP. These platform teams are T-shaped teams that have expertise in cloud engineering, security, networking, compliance, and so forth. In many enterprises, these domain experts are not used to working on the same team with shared incentives.

Successful platform teams treat the cloud platform as a product, and shift from *project*-centric thinking to *product*-centric thinking. This mindshift change introduces new skill sets for the organization.

Here is an example. A large retailer that we'll call BoxMart created a platform team to offer basic AWS services for its development teams. The platform team had the following roles (remember, a role does not equal a person):

- Platform architect
- Security engineer
- Infrastructure engineer
- Operations engineer
- IT automation engineer (DevOps engineer)

The team released the first generation of its platform with basic IaaS services to satisfy the requirements for BoxMart's first cloud applications. (This kind of release is known as *minimal viable cloud*, or MVC.) The first few workloads were simple three-tier web apps.

Next, they planned out MVC2, and many of the targeted workloads were in the area of analytics and machine learning. They added Samantha, an analytics engineer, to the mix who has broad knowledge of cloud computing, infrastructure, and machine learning, and deep knowledge of analytics and big data. Samantha's expertise had a very different T shape than that of the other team members, but collectively, the platform team now had all the skills it would need for MVC2. She began training on the cloud platform ("broadening her personal T") while training the others on her analytics and machine learning expertise (her I-shaped knowledge), broadening the team's collective T-shaped knowledge.

When Samantha joined the team, the platform owner, Eduardo, worked with human resources to change Samantha's goals and objectives to match those of the platform. Samantha still had some specific goals and objectives for her area of expertise (her "I"), but now she also had goals and objectives in common with her new teammates. This is an important step because she now has incentives based on the overall success of the platform, not just the success of her area of expertise. This drives higher degrees of collaboration and sharing; it takes an entire team to be successful. With her old incentives, she could meet her goals even if the team fell short. This can lead to the "it's not my job" behavior so common in silo-based organizations.

In addition to a broad range of technical skills, teams also need soft skills as they move toward a product-centric model with T-shaped teams. Like Samantha, Eduardo, and the entire platform team, your team will need strong communication skills, empathy, and product development skills, and you'll need to create shared goals and objectives to keep everyone aligned.

Using product development skills within IT is a new concept to many organizations. Sure, IT people are accustomed to having product owners, but what I'm talking about is shifting away from *project*-based development to *product*-based development. With project-based development, teams are driven by a due date and a budget. The focus is on how many features can be delivered in a given time frame. Product-based development is more long-term, with a focus on outcomes, not features. In his book *Project to Product* (IT Revolution Press), Mik Kersten contrasts the success factors for project- versus product-based development. Project-based development uses a cost center approach: it's all about being on time and on budget. Accounting capitalizes all of the development work, which results in large projects and business owners asking for everything they need up front.

Product-based development, by contrast, takes a profit center approach. People are measured based on business objectives and outcomes, such as increased sales, customer retention, new customers, and improved profit margins. This approach drives shorter, more iterative development processes as product teams want to see business value sooner. How many user stories, which features, and what velocity you have are not as important as whether customers are satisfied, how many new customers register, and whether the company exceeds its planned revenue numbers for the quarter.

Their measures of success are just one way that product-based approaches differ from project-based approaches. Kersten highlights seven key differences. The bottom line here is that one of the biggest advantages of cloud computing is agility, but a project-based approach to software development will make it much harder to achieve faster speed to market in the cloud. We have to change our approach to how we build and run software to maximize the benefits of cloud.

Cloud Is Bigger than Just IT

Many people think that cloud computing is an IT project, but its arc of influence and organizational impact reach far beyond the IT department to every part of the company. It is critical to be aware of these impacts—if you aren't, you risk major setbacks in cloud adoption. Table 3-1 shows a high-level summary of how cloud computing impacts various departments.

Table 3-1. How departments outside of IT experience change during the cloud adoption journey

Department	What is changing?
Finance	Shift from capital expenditures (CAPEX) to operating expenditures (OPEX)
Procurement	Shift from licenses and maintenance fees to subscription models
Legal	Moving to a shared responsibility model, data ownership
Human Resources	New skills, recruiting models, operating model changes
Sales	Shift from shrink-wrapped product to always-on services

AUDITING AND FINANCE

Auditors can drastically slow down cloud adoption. Most auditors are not technical. Of those who are, few understand cloud computing well enough to realize that the methods they use to audit physical datacenters are suboptimal or even invalid for auditing cloud services. I have seen auditors demand access to a CSP's datacenters in order to perform a valid audit. This makes no sense in the public cloud for two reasons. First, the CSP's datacenters host applications and data for many customers. If I am a bank, the last thing I want is my competitors' auditors walking the raised floor at AWS or Microsoft where my bank's assets are running. Second, there is no tangible place that holds a customer's assets for an auditor to even look at. Those cloud assets aren't sitting on the raised floor in your datacenter; they're distributed through many nodes across multiple datacenters externally, and it is impossible to know exactly which ones.

I have even seen auditors flat out refuse to allow a company to use public cloud services because they could not "walk the floor" of the datacenter. This is bizarre. The job of the auditor is not to dictate technology; it's to ensure compliance with whatever regulations the company has committed to. To keep auditing from becoming a major bottleneck, companies need to educate auditors about the shared responsibility model and help them refine their processes to be more cloud friendly.

Responsibility for physical infrastructure lies with the CSPs. They have their own audits and must be certified by various regulatory bodies. Their customers' auditors have access to these audit reports and certifications and can decide whether they are acceptable. Table 3-2 shows a sampling of compliance programs that companies adhere to.

Table 3-2. Common compliance programs

Compliance program	Description
PCI DSS	Payment Card Industry Data Security Standard
SOC 2	Service Organization Control 2
GDPR	General Data Protection Regulation (EU)
FedRAMP	Federal Risk and Authorization Management Program
FERPA	Family Educational Rights and Privacy Act
HIPAA	Health Insurance Portability and Accountability Act
G-Cloud	UK Government Cloud controls
ITAR	International Traffic in Arms Regulations

Similarly, finance and accounting departments have processes that were designed for buying and depreciating physical assets over time. The cloud is a pay-as-you-go, consumption-based model and is classified as an operating expense.

Budgeting and forecasting infrastructure costs are very different as well. Accounting departments are used to forecasting the company's infrastructure needs at the beginning of a fiscal year. They may budget for two or three times the expected capacity to handle demand spikes or growth over the course of the year. Once the budget is allocated, everyone works within it. If the actual numbers vary greatly from the forecasted numbers, departments may have to request additional funds, and the finance department can choose whether or not to allocate those funds.

In a consumption-based model, you don't have that choice: you pay for what you use. The advantage of this model is that you don't have to buy two or three times the capacity to be able to handle spikes or growth. The downside is that if your systems consume five times the forecasted amount, you have to pay for it.

PROCUREMENT

Let me tell you two stories that show how procurement departments can seriously hinder cloud adoption if they don't plan and prepare properly.

My first story concerns a large financial institution, which we'll call Oxford Bank. Oxford had six months to implement the first version of its cloud platform (MVC 1) and migrate the first two applications to it. The first three months of the project were spent assessing Oxford's security, operations, and DevOps maturity to identify the technology, people, and process gaps the company needed to fill. The next three months were for the actual build-out. In month four, Oxford's architects decided to move to a third-party SaaS-based logging solution instead of the legacy on-premises solution it was currently using. The problem was that Oxford's procurement process for new vendors took at least six months, which would significantly delay the project. But because that process was outside the IT department, no one considered it in planning the cloud transition. The CTO didn't even know about this policy until the project suddenly faced a major delay.

This procurement model had been set in stone for decades. It was a relic of a much slower-moving time. To ensure enough time to integrate the solution into the logging framework of the cloud platform, the CTO had to push the organization to change its procurement process to one that would move much more quickly. The CTO made a lot of progress: Oxford approved the SaaS solution in a month. This was better, but it still delayed the project by a month.

Had the CTO been aware of this problem beforehand, they could have started addressing the procurement issue during the three-month assessment phase rather than waiting until the build-out period had already begun, avoiding the delay.

Such communication gaps can create serious problems. It's important to make sure all stakeholders are included before moving any workload to the cloud. The moral of this story is: when taking on any large cloud project, understand all of your dependencies from other groups outside of IT and assess if there are any blockers due to legacy processes or outdated best practices.

The second story I'll tell you is another cautionary tale.

Back in 2014, a logistics company (let's call it ABC Logistics) had its logistics platform installed in its customers' datacenters; the customers paid for customizations to the platform. The customers no longer wanted to deal with these painful upgrades and customization efforts; they just wanted to consume the logistics services as SaaS. To provide this, ABC wanted to migrate its core application to the public cloud.

So IT started migrating the application—but no one consulted the rest of the company. The sales department had structured all of its incentives around selling the customized services that this migration would make obsolete. Furthermore,

ABC had a very large organization of technicians who onboarded clients, performed upgrades onsite, and provided customer-facing support for the logistics platform.

When these teams got wind of the IT plan and learned that it was already in process, all hell broke loose. Moving to a SaaS model was a major organizational change for these non-IT departments, yet only IT had been consulted! This pushback derailed the entire initiative for quite some time; eventually, ABC restarted the project as an enterprise initiative instead of an IT initiative.

ABC Logistics learned the hard way that the impact of changing its delivery would be much broader than just within IT. Oxford Bank and ABC Logistics both performed admirably from a technology standpoint, but suffered delays because they hadn't considered how the cloud transition would affect how people were incentivized and trained to perform their current tasks. Oxford was able to mitigate the impact and it only cost the company a month. At ABC, not only did this cost the company several months, it torpedoed morale, and the company had to deal with the fallout for a long time.

Just like in the previous story, factors outside of IT derailed ABC's cloud initiative. When moving or building new workloads in the cloud, assess the impact on the *entire* organization to prevent any surprises that could bring your cloud journey to a halt.

CLOUD SERVICE AGREEMENTS

Another huge bottleneck is the cloud provider agreements. I have seen enterprises and CSPs battle it out between their lawyers for months on end to come to terms on the agreement. The CSPs do not budge much from their terms, and the enterprise lawyers usually don't understand the shared responsibility model. Cloud service agreements (CSAs) are made up of three artifacts: the customer agreement, the acceptable use policy (AUP), and the service-level agreement (SLA).

The *customer agreement* describes the overall relationship between the customer and the CSP. It includes the processes and procedures used by the cloud provider, explicit definitions of the roles, responsibilities, and execution of various processes. This is the area where there is some flexibility in the terms.

The *AUP* prohibits activities that providers consider to be an improper or outright illegal use of their service. This is one area of a CSA where there is considerable consistency across cloud providers. The language in this section is similar across vendors and is mostly nonnegotiable.

SLAs describe levels of service in areas such as availability, serviceability, or performance. The SLA specifies thresholds and financial penalties associated with violations of these thresholds. The SLAs are mostly nonnegotiable, but the penalties and incident response actions have room for negotiations. SLAs in the cloud are very different from what lawyers and procurement managers are used to. In the cloud, the SLAs are set for a given service: for example, Table 3-3 shows the SLAs and service credits percentages of the AWS compute service called EC2 (*https://aws.amazon.com/compute/sla*).

Table 3-3. SLAs and service credit percentages for EC2

Monthly uptime percentage	Service credit percentage
Less than 99.99% but equal to or greater than 99.0%	10%
Less than 99.0% but equal to or greater than 95.0%	30%
Less than 95.0%	100%

In this example, AWS is only responsible for the SLA of that service, not of your application(s) that uses it. In fact, AWS and the other providers provide numerous resources such as training, whitepapers, knowledge bases, and other content to help you build highly redundant architectures that can exceed the AWS SLAs.

This is why procurement and legal experts need to be trained in cloud computing and understand the differences between an agreement for a cloud service versus an agreement for a shrink-wrapped software package or physical hardware.

Talent Strategies

Companies often overlook recruiting, retaining, and training staff when planning and budgeting for a large cloud initiative. The enterprise leaders driving the cloud transformation need to work closely with their human capital team to design and build the right talent strategy. Here are some things to consider.

Gartner journalist Meghan Rimol estimates (*https://www.gartner.com/smarter withgartner/4-trends-impacting-cloud-adoption-in-2020*) that "insufficient cloud IaaS skills will delay half of enterprise IT organizations' migration to the cloud by two years or more." She notes that many cloud migration strategies are geared toward "lift-and-shift" as opposed to modernization or refactoring, an approach that results in less development of cloud native skills among staff.

There is a shortage of cloud talent both within the enterprise and within the consulting industry. Companies have to leverage multiple approaches to find the right people, including training within, hiring from outside, and working with system integrators and managed service providers.

RECRUIT

Experienced cloud talent is hard to find. Once employees have cloud skills and experience, every recruiter under the sun starts knocking on their door. Many people will tell you that enjoying their work is more important than salary, but companies are making offers many skilled cloud professionals just can't refuse. It is a classic supply-and-demand problem that isn't likely to disappear anytime soon.

Your human capital team should be very good at building recruiting strategies, but they'll need your help. Provide them with training on cloud computing so they know, at minimum, the value proposition of cloud for the company and have a sense of what all the terms mean. Second, they'll need your help defining all of the roles and job descriptions required for the cloud. Third, they'll need your ideas on where to find talent. Are there conferences or local events that they should be attending? What specific sets of hard and soft skills are you looking for? How much work can be done remotely and how much will have to be on site?

Include someone from human capital on your cloud leadership team from day one. Make them part of the journey. They can help build out training, retainment, and recruiting plans iteratively, and participating will keep them in sync with the progress of the overall cloud transformation. This is important because when the hiring requirements start to scale up, the recruiting team needs to be ready.

TRAIN

One thing that companies leading successful cloud adoption initiatives have in common is that they make a significant financial commitment to training their employees and give them strong incentives to earn cloud certifications. Some companies partner with online training vendors that offer subscription services. (Cloud Academy, Cloud Guru, and Coursera are a few of the leaders in this space.) The cloud service providers also offer training programs. These programs teach employees how to build and run workloads in the cloud, but what they don't teach is how cloud is done within *your* organization. Every organization has its own processes, policies, and controls and its own cloud strategy, all of which play an important role in cloud technology decisions.

The most successful companies create enterprise-wide internal training programs, or "tech colleges," that combine online training from vendors with significant homegrown training content, fully staffed with instructors and content creators. They offer these training programs not just to engineering but to the entire company. This requires a substantial investment, but the benefits are many:

- Upskill talent

- Consistent messaging and branding

- Morale booster

- Increases cloud adoption

- Increases certifications

- Attracts new talent

A big part of cloud adoption is communicating the overall vision. Why should each employee care about the cloud transition? Internal training programs provide an opportunity to communicate the overall vision each time an employee enters a training class. Training isn't just for technologists. The more cloud-savvy your non-IT people are, the more effective they'll be when working with their IT counterparts and their customers.

Internal training programs should have two major focus areas. The first is upskilling employees for the cloud; the second is constantly communicating the company's cloud vision, strategy, and cultural messaging. These are critical. Organizational-change guru John Kotter calls this the "WIIFM": "What's in it for me?"[1] If people don't know their WIIFM, it can be challenging to get them to buy into the vision and thus to the organizational changes needed.

Delivering training too soon or too late is counterproductive. Some companies rush to train a large number of employees before there is actual cloud-related work to do. By the time they finally get assigned to a project that leverages cloud technologies, many will have forgotten what they learned in training. Other companies don't plan for training up front but, when the surge of cloud-related

---

1 John P. Kotter, *Leading Change* (Harvard Business Review Press).

projects hits, rush people off to training in the hope that they will be productive on day one.

The best approach is a training plan that grounds people in the concepts of cloud computing early, but coordinates the more technical classes with developers nearing the start of their cloud projects. This gives them time to take what they learned and get some hands-on experience in a safe, low-pressure environment before racing off to start a project.

RETAIN

During the dot-com days of the 1990s, when startups were hiring engineering talent at a record pace, they rolled out the perks: free food, laundry services, foosball tables, and more. That is obviously nice, but it's not the talent-retention strategy I'm talking about.

What most developers want is to get their work done at "cloud speed." The legacy processes and legacy thinking this book discusses are obstacles in the way of getting code out the door. If you want to retain talent, don't make their job so damn hard.

For example, spinning up an environment on your own account on any public cloud provider takes minutes. Large enterprises need a little more process to ensure that new environments are brought up safely and in compliance, and that resources aren't left on indefinitely (which can spike cloud spending). But too often I have seen the process of requesting an environment take weeks or even months. Even worse, these environments can be so locked down that the developer can't get work done without constantly opening tickets. This can become such a source of frustration that people will actually leave.

One strategy to combat this frustration is to implement programs focusing on continuous improvement and productivity. These programs should not be run as command-and-control structures but as communities, where the people doing the work collaborate on ways to improve productivity. When people feel that they are heard and that they can make a difference, they are more likely to stay. Tactics like lunch and learn events, internal technology webinars, tech blogging, and writing whitepapers are just some ways that companies provide mechanisms for employees to share and learn from each other.

Dojos are also a great way for employees to share what they learn. The Japanese word *dojo* comes from martial arts; in karate, the dojo is the central location where students meet for extensive, immersive training with masters.

One company that has set the standard for implementing Dojos is Target. Target understood early on that the pace of innovation in retail was moving at lightning speed, and to continue to compete in this space, they would need to shift to an engineering mindset. As they set out to embrace concepts new to Target employees like cloud, Agile, Lean, product mindset, and DevOps, they implemented Dojos as an immersive learning environment to teach teams the new ways of working. What was unique with Target's approach is that the teams would work on actual projects. As they learned, they applied that learning to their actual sprint, making the learning experience much more relevant than the traditional methods. Dojos are great not only for training, but are also a great way to drive culture change.

Experienced cloud developers want jobs where they can learn and share information. Jobs that allow developers to hone their skills are very rewarding and help keep them relevant in the marketplace. Events like DevOpsDays, cloud meetups, and hackathons create great learning, sharing, and networking opportunities. Maintaining an external tech blog, allowing people to contribute to open source projects, and encouraging public speaking at conferences are other ways to add value to employee careers and working experience.

Experts who don't get ample opportunity to leverage their cloud skills are experts who walk out the door. I have seen talented cloud architects, people who want to be building new cloud native apps or replatforming legacy applications on the cloud, get stuck doing repetitive "lift and shift to the cloud" work. There are people who love that kind of work and others who despise it. Make sure you know where a person sits on that spectrum before you assign them to an 18-month cloud migration project.

Then there's salary. Cloud skills are in high demand, and that is reflected in the average salaries of cloud architects, security engineers, SREs, and DevOps engineers. The cloud leadership team should work with human capital leadership to evaluate the company pay scale and make sure that everyone is being fairly compensated. You may also want to adjust the compensation packages of your key contributors, because companies are searching high and low for cloud talent.

Finally, evaluate the wellness of your staff. Burnout was a huge problem in the IT industry before the Covid-19 pandemic, and issues with remote work, childcare, and quarantine restrictions have made the situation worse. People are working around the clock, over the weekends, and through their vacations and family time. Put programs in place to evaluate the health and wellness of your staff and encourage work-life balance.

Many companies offer employee health and wellness programs that educate and provide help with topics like how to deal with stress, mental health problems, and addiction; managing weight and nutrition; and caring for children and elders. Some even offer on-site childcare, flexible hours, vaccination clinics, gym memberships, and other benefits. Other programs focus on community involvement, teamwork, and mentorship. Sometimes just creating an event to break up the monotony of the day-to-day grind can help employees refresh and de-stress. These might include team sports, talent shows, tech conferences, and book clubs.

Conclusion

People are the most important part of the cloud adoption journey—and the hardest. People perform better when they have a vested interest in the outcome, in terms of both the company's performance and their own personal development. The job market for experienced cloud talent is hot, and your employees have lots of options. As part of your cloud journey, make sure you create an environment that creates psychological safety, provides resources for employees to train and grow, and, most importantly, removes the obstacles that make it hard for people to do their jobs.

4

Process

As you've seen throughout the book so far, legacy processes can stifle agility and innovation because they were designed in a different era, with different constraints, when the infrastructure you ran your software on could be seen and touched.

Cloud practitioners need to rethink how we work. As you learned in Chapter 1, we also need to build trust into our systems so we can get rid of all those low-value, time-consuming review gates blocking our way.

But where do we start?

A company I'll call NCC Enterprises outsourced its infrastructure provisioning and management to a third party. In the datacenter, the SLA for procuring and provisioning new infrastructure was three months. The process required several forms and approvals before an order was placed. Once the infrastructure equipment the vendor had ordered arrived, NCC put the provisioning process in a backlog and completed all of its higher-priority provisioning jobs first. Thus, the SLA contained a lot of padding to account for large queues and emergency requests that might take a higher priority. Sometimes, if you got lucky, you might get your infrastructure installed in two months, but often it was three or more.

When NCC decided to start leveraging the cloud, the provisioning process did not change. The requesters still had to fill out forms and get approvals. The ticket was still processed by the third party and fell into the same queue as the physical infrastructure, even though installing the infrastructure was only a matter of running a script. Several months later, some of NCC's business leaders started questioning the value of cloud computing because they had not seen an improvement in turnaround time.

The Software Development Life Cycle

To understand the breadth of processes that make up the software development life cycle (SDLC), let's look at an Information Technology Infrastructure Library (ITIL) framework diagram (Figure 4-1).[1] It's a great visual representation of what goes into building and running software.

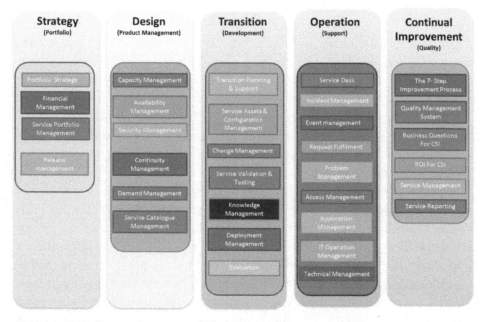

Figure 4-1. ITIL framework, courtesy of ITIL (https://commons.wikimedia.org/w/index.php?curid=41897813)

As you can see, there are lots of steps in the SDLC. Going through them all would be well outside the scope of this book, so in this chapter I'll focus on service transition and service operations, two of the SDLC steps that require the most change to optimize for cloud. These services can particularly hinder cloud adoption if the legacy processes are not reengineered for the cloud, and they have an enormous impact on the ability to deliver software to cloud endpoints.

---

1 I am neither endorsing nor condoning ITIL (*https://www.itlibrary.org*), which is a library of best practices for managing IT services and improving IT support and service levels. One of its main goals is to ensure that IT services align with business objectives, even as business objectives change.

In the legacy model, each process in Figure 4-1 is usually owned by a group. Each group has a *process flow*, or a sequence of processes, for receiving, processing, and completing requests. If you add up all the boxes, it becomes evident that there is a lot of process to navigate to get software out the door. Figure 4-2 shows a suboptimal process flow for building and deploying software. You can see plenty of manual processes, handoffs, and review gates.

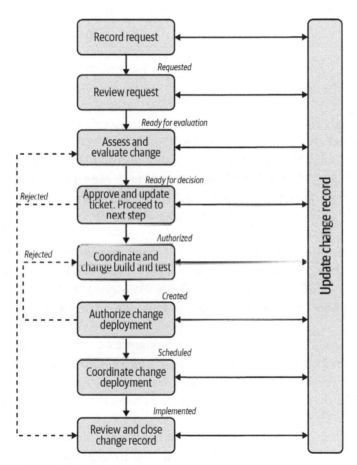

Figure 4-2. Suboptimal software-deployment process flow

Automation can greatly reduce the time it takes to deploy software. In Figure 4-3, you can see that many of those manual processes, handoffs, and review gates have been replaced by high levels of automation in the CI/CD pipeline. Where companies often go wrong is that they put little thought into redesigning those existing processes to optimize the flow of work. They try to simply automate their existing processes, but end up automating all of the bottle-necks and waste within them.

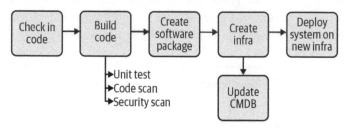

Figure 4-3. An automated CI/CD pipeline

This kind of automation effort ensures that deploying software in the cloud will not go well. It's the equivalent of the VP of Electricity from Chapter 1 making everyone fill out forms and obtain permissions instead of just putting a plug into an outlet. Sure, the VP of Electricity still needs to provide high SLAs for the electricity services and to make sure there are redundant sources of power, but that should all be abstracted from the power consumers, who only care that the outlet in the wall works.

Just as consuming electricity as a service requires a different model than producing it with your own generators and turbines, consuming computing as a service requires a different model. If you don't acknowledge and embrace the need to rethink processes, you're setting up your enterprise's cloud adoption for failure.

Under *service transition*, there are a few processes that can easily become huge bottlenecks if they are not optimized for the cloud. The first is *change management*, the process of identifying changes to both infrastructure and software. The point of change management is to understand the impacts, dependencies, and risks associated with the changes and address them to minimize disruption to services. *Release and deployment management* is the process of ensuring the integrity of the production environment and confirming that the correct components are released. This includes planning, building, testing, deploying, and accessing the software and production environments. *Service validation and testing* assesses the impact and benefits of the changes, to ensure operations can support the new services.

Under *service operations*, the potential major bottleneck areas are access management (determining permissions and limiting access to authorized users only), incident management (restoring services to the users as quickly as possible when systems become unreliable), and problem management (analyzing incidents to prevent new ones). I'll discuss the kinds of optimization required in Part II of the book.

This chapter will discuss methods of reengineering processes to improve the flow of work and reduce process bottlenecks. I'll introduce the concept of *value stream mapping* (VSM), which is a method used to analyze existing processes and redesign them for optimal flow. VSM is a Lean management tool commonly used by companies that are far along in their DevOps maturity.

Process optimization, also called process reengineering, can be a daunting task. Changing processes can challenge cultural norms, impact existing roles and responsibilities, and require structural changes to the organization to optimize flow. Changes in process can be met with resistance, especially in workplace cultures where change is infrequent or even unwelcome.

My advice is to start at the biggest pain point. If your organization is early in its cloud journey, that's usually one of four areas: environment provisioning, deployment processes, incident management, and security processes.

I'll look at each of these four process areas in turn, then examine how value stream mapping can help you optimize them for cloud.

ENVIRONMENT PROVISIONING

In the public cloud, infrastructure is code, not physical machines or appliances. Provisioning infrastructure and environments in the public cloud can be accomplished in minutes. Obviously, you need to make sure infrastructure is provisioned in a cost-effective, secure, and compliant manner—but that shouldn't add days, weeks, or months to the timeline. So how do you balance control with agility? Let me illustrate with the experience of one of my consulting clients. Here's how a legacy process almost killed a large media company's cloud initiative.

MediaCo used to be a traditional waterfall shop: it progressed through the SDLC one phase at a time. All test environments were run on-premises on shared physical infrastructure in the datacenter. Two system administrators were responsible for maintaining the test environments. With the start of each new release cycle, they had to wipe all test environments clean and refresh the databases. They scheduled this process for the end of each month, which forced project teams to schedule their sprints and releases around the refresh events. If there were any unplanned outages or if emergency fixes or patches were needed, none of the development teams could test until the test environments were brought back online.

This process worked well for MediaCo for many years because its development teams released biannually or quarterly. There was plenty of time to plan and coordinate the refresh process. But as they became more mature in practicing Agile, development teams were moving to more frequent releases, putting more strain on the two system administrators who had to keep up with all of their requests.

At the same time, MediaCo was looking at ways to leverage the public cloud, and the dynamic nature of the test environments was an attractive use case. So it decided to migrate its test environments to the public cloud. The problem was, the infrastructure team viewed the public cloud as just "someone else's datacenter" and tried to apply the exact same tools and processes they'd used in their own datacenter.

To make matters worse, the business units declared that they no longer wanted to work in a shared environment because they were tired of being delayed by other project teams' schedules and testing cycles. This created even more work for the system administrators, who would now have to manage multiple infrastructure environments.

MediaCo was heading for a failed cloud migration—until my team challenged them to rethink their business processes.

Processes don't come from nowhere. They are created to fulfill a need: a set of requirements, as set forth in company policies. When we asked the MediaCo administrators what the actual policies were that drove their process, they kept referring to the process itself. They were focused on the "how," not the "why." Once we got them to stop thinking about the existing process and start defining their actual *requirements,* which were mostly driven by the security and compliance teams, things started getting easier.

The real requirements were:

- Test environments must be refreshed on a defined interval.
- All personally identifiable information (PII) must be masked in the test environment.
- Access to the environment must be granted on a "need-to-know" basis.
- Test environments must not allow public access.

There were other requirements, but those were the four major ones. Unfortunately, the way MediaCo was fulfilling those requirements was creating huge inefficiencies. More than a dozen development teams were sitting idle for three to five days out of every month, waiting for the refresh to be executed. That is an extraordinary amount of waste and lost productivity. MediaCo was preparing to duplicate that same process in the cloud, which would have created zero value for its customers, the developers. (I'll talk more about why you should view the developers as your customers in Part II of this book.)

Here's what wasn't on that list of requirements: that the two system administrators who ran the test environment had to be the ones to do the refresh. There was no reason they couldn't create the code to automate the tasks, then allow the development teams to run the refresh themselves once they obtained the proper approvals.

It took a while to get everyone to look past their current processes and see that there was a better way. To make this point clear, we conducted a value stream mapping workshop that allowed them to see the bottlenecks in the existing process. We then worked with them to redesign the entire process in a way that was optimized for the cloud and for self provisioning.

The result was that development teams no longer had to work their sprint plans around an artificial refresh date each month, and they no longer lost days of development and testing time. The system administrators were no longer a bottleneck; they didn't have to work 80 hours a week trying to keep up with all of the requests. And MediaCo could now leverage the cloud to spin up environments on demand and turn them off when not in use (off hours, weekends, holidays, etc.), which ended up saving the company over a million dollars.

This was a tremendous success for MediaCo, and it opened the doors to more opportunities in the public cloud. Had MediaCo not redesigned its existing processes, its implementation in the cloud may have cost even more than what it had in its datacenter. Another win for the company was that the new design improved morale for the two system administrators, who were no longer overworked and underappreciated; the developers, who were more productive; and the product owners, who were now getting their new features on time.

As we move to the cloud and embrace a more iterative approach to software development, many of our former "best practices" are now nothing more than process bottlenecks. In an age where speed to market is a competitive advantage, we need to take a step back and rethink our value streams.

Once again, we need to focus on what the requirements are that drove the existing processes, not the actual process implementation. Focus on the why, not the how. Why do we have so many review meetings? The answer is that we need to enforce coding standards and architecture best practices. We need to access risks from a security, compliance, and impact standpoint. We need to ensure that proper performance and regression testing are performed. The list goes on.

DEPLOYMENT PROCESSES

A common problem I see play out at many companies is they take their existing deployment "best practices" with them to the cloud. Often, the deployment processes were originally designed in an era when large monolithic applications were deployed on physical infrastructure biannually or quarterly. The process often consists of several manual steps, including numerous review meetings, approvals, forms to fill out, and checklists.

A better way to approach this is to understand what the required policies, controls, and standards are and automate the review process by adding tools like code scans into the CI/CD process. CI/CD, as you'll recall from Chapter 3, allows us to automate the software deployment process from end to end, with no human intervention. These tools are configured to look for coding standards, security policies, and audit controls, and can fail the build process if a certain threshold of security, quality, and compliance is not achieved. The build process can also be configured to automatically update any enterprise asset management system or configuration management database (CMDB).

The power of CI/CD lies in automation. If you are allowed to rethink how your company delivers software, you can get extremely creative on how to leverage CI/CD to streamline your IT processes. CI/CD pipelines can eliminate a lot of manual reviews and checkpoints that are primarily in place because of a lack of trust.

Why this lack of trust in automation? One of the main reasons is that deployment is traditionally full of manual, nonrepeatable processes. People have been burned so often by botched deployments that they have inserted numerous process steps to try to add more trust in the deployment process. With a good CI/CD pipeline that is fully automated, auditable, and repeatable, we can start trusting our automation and removing some of the process obstacles that prevent us from delivering faster.

A few of the aspects of pipelines that can be fully automated are:

- Builds
- Code scans for enforcing best practices, including:
    - Coding standards
    - Cloud architecture best practices

— Security policy enforcement

— Compliance controls enforcement

- Creating a cloud environment with mandated guardrails for security and compliance
- Updating the configuration management database for asset tracking
- Creating metadata and tagging for infrastructure
- Code deployment and rollback, as needed

These automated processes can supply all of the necessary documentation required for auditing. But automation giveth, and automation taketh away: it gives us a standard and repeatable process that can increase quality, security hygiene, compliance, and delivery velocity—but takes away the tasks, committees, meetings, checklists, and other manual things that are part of people's jobs. What often happens is the team that builds out the CI/CD pipeline only automates the steps that are in their control; they still have to "prove" the deployment is ready by attending meetings and filling out forms and checklists.

A large financial company I'll call Prosperity embraced the concepts of CI/CD within its development process and found that its team could perform a build and create the supporting infrastructure in minutes with the push of a button. The problem was, the rest of the company was not ready to embrace this level of automation because they didn't trust it.

In response, Prosperity decided to perform a *value stream mapping* (VSM) exercise. In a VSM exercise, you interview all of the stakeholders and participants in a particular unit of work so that you can visualize all of the steps required to complete it. This makes it easier to find lag time or waste. Once you identify the problems, the goal is to redesign the process to optimize the flow and reduce waste.

The unit of work Prosperity analyzed was "build a brand-new application." Prosperity interviewed numerous stakeholders and mapped out the current state process, which filled one entire wall of a conference room. What it revealed was that, before a developer could launch that lightning-fast CI/CD process, they had to navigate 60 to 90 days of manual steps: tickets, emails, and verbal communication for approvals, access requests, account creation, accounting code creations, and so on. Much of that 60 to 90 days was wait time: the process stalled as everyone waited for the next step to be completed.

After that initial setup and approval stage, the development team could create and build the new software quickly. They were allowed to use CI/CD to push the code to a nonproduction environment. The CI/CD process included automated tests, code scans for standards and best practices, and code scans for security policies. If the code did not pass the requirements for quality, standards, and security, the build would fail. If it did pass, the code was put in staging and ready for production.

The VSM showed, however, that after this fast and efficient stage, there was another 60 to 90 days of process focusing on reviews and approvals—even though the automation had already proved that the code met all of the requirements to deploy to production. In other words, regardless of the product or feature requirements and no matter how good their CI/CD process was, any change at all would take four to six months!

Prosperity's use case reveals why it is so important to look at how technology changes affect people and processes. Most manual review gates and approvals can be automated and result in better security, compliance, and quality than the manual review process. At the same time, the time to market can be drastically improved, providing more business value to customers.

INCIDENT MANAGEMENT

Incident management for software in the public cloud must be redesigned, because the underlying infrastructure, from the hypervisor down, is now the responsibility of the CSPs. (Refer to the shared responsibility model from Figure 1-2.) Your responsibility is to monitor the CSP and work with them to resolve any issues that stem from the infrastructure layer.

You can see in Figure 4-4 that the cloud platform team is responsible for the SLAs of the cloud platform, and the developers are responsible for the operations of their applications built on top of the platform. (In Chapter 5 and 6, I'll look more closely at cloud platforms as an internal CSP that delivers cloud services to the development teams.) If you don't optimize your incident management process for the cloud, you could run into problems.

Shared responsibility model as an internal cloud provider

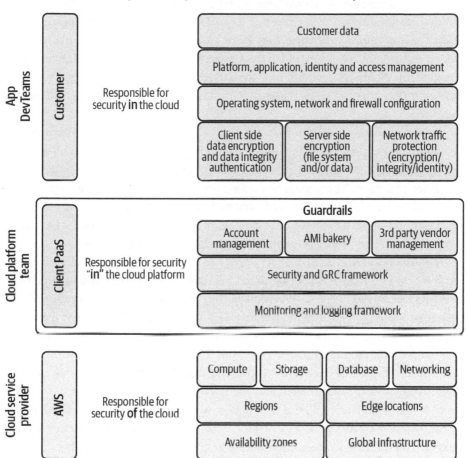

Figure 4-4. The platform's role as an internal cloud provider within the shared responsibility model

I worked with a Fortune 100 company (we'll call it MegaCorp) that was an early adopter of both cloud computing and DevOps. The infrastructure team built a cloud platform on top of a private cloud and worked with the security, compliance, and development teams to embed policies and controls in the cloud platform while adding scanning capabilities to the CI/CD process. They did a great job of rethinking and automating their provisioning and deployment processes—but they did not redesign any of their operational processes.

MegaCorp's cloud journey started out successfully. One of the largest companies on the planet was now able to take a new business requirement and deploy it to production in a matter of days. The security and compliance teams trusted the automation because they knew that the build would fail if it did not meet the stringent requirements of their heavily regulated industry. The feedback was glowing. Business partners who were used to waiting months to get new features were now seeing daily releases of mobile and web capabilities. So far, so good!

It was nirvana—until the first incident. Then things got ugly. The incident management process was still working with a legacy design, in which all support and operations were centrally managed within domain silos. The help desk provided tier 1 support. There were ops teams for networking, databases, infrastructure, and so on. When an incident occurred, a ticket was created and routed to tier 1 support—but they were only capable of solving basic problems like password resets, so they would route the ticket to the development team.

The development team had no access to servers or logs, so when a ticket came in, they'd create a *new* ticket to get log data for the timeframe in which the event had occurred. This took several hours. Once they had a snapshot of the logs, they could start solving the mystery. If someone had a hunch that there was something wrong with the database performance, they'd open up yet another ticket and route it to the database team. And then they'd wait. Eventually the database team would come back and recommend that the network team look into the issue. *Another* ticket was created and *more* wait time ensued. Incidents bounced around the organization like a hot potato while business users waited impatiently. After a couple of weeks of long resolution times, the excitement went away and business partners started asking to go back to the old model.

This was not a problem with the cloud; this was an ineffective process. We helped the client implement a logging and monitoring framework into their cloud platform that gave the developers self-service access to logs and application performance monitoring tools, without having to log on to servers. After fine-tuning the new incident management process, the product team quickly got their mean time to repair back to an acceptable level and eventually won back the trust of their customers.

The biggest lesson I learned on this project was that, even though the client did everything right by redesigning the provisioning and deployment processes, leveraging their existing operations processes almost killed their cloud project.

Had they chosen to pilot with a mission-critical application, they might not have recovered so easily—or ever.

SECURITY PROCESSES

Security teams spend years mitigating risks and monitoring for threats to protect their employers' crown jewels. But the tooling and processes that work well to secure a datacenter don't translate well to securing cloud services. The security policies and requirements are still valid, but implementing them in the cloud is very different.

I worked with a large enterprise in a highly regulated industry; we'll call it Nightingale Health. Before this company's architects could migrate any applications to the cloud, they had to prove to the CISO that the cloud platform they were building was at least as secure as their existing datacenter. Nightingale had recently completed a network segmentation project on-prem and the network team was demanding that the cloud platform team leverage the exact same design for network segmentation in the public cloud. This would be much harder than leveraging the CSP's cloud native security APIs. For example, on AWS, platform teams use a virtual private cloud (VPC) with public and private subnets to accomplish the equivalent of network segmentation on-prem. Unfortunately, Nightingale's network team was insisting on a more complex design, including buying software appliances to be installed on the public cloud.

The platform architects did not feel empowered to challenge the network architects' decisions. They tried their best to architect a public cloud solution that closely mimicked the on-prem implementation. When I challenged the platform team's design, one architect responded, "I know it's the wrong thing to do, but we don't have a choice."

I asked the network team for their requirements, but they sent me a document that looked more like a design, complete with solutions and vendor names. I was asking them about the "why," but they were giving me the "how." Eventually, we broke through and got to the real requirements that drove their network segmentation strategy. Then my team proposed a cloud native design to meet those requirements. Eventually that design was accepted and implemented, which saved Nightingale from implementing a very expensive, complex, and inefficient solution.

Security teams, like other teams, need to separate requirements from implementation—the "why" from the "how." Then they need to be open to satisfying their requirements in new ways that are more optimal for the cloud.

The entire approach to security should change in the cloud. Many security policies can be baked into the underlying infrastructure. Others can be enforced through code scans in the CI/CD process. Continuous security monitoring can raise alerts immediately when someone isn't adhering to security policies, so that quick action can minimize the exposure window. By now you're familiar with the term *infrastructure as code*, but you should also be thinking of *security as code*. The more you automate and continuously monitor your security policies, the less you'll need to deal with forms, meetings, and manual approvals, so you can bring products, features, and fixes to market much faster.

The most important advice I can give about security processes is this: people who design and mandate security-related processes should first pass a cloud certification on their cloud provider of choice, or they should already have extensive experience on a successful cloud transformation. If neither of these is true, the odds of their processes being well suited for building, deploying, and running software in the cloud are very low. People with no cloud experience and without enough training to pass a certification often tend to think of the cloud as "somebody else's datacenter." When people say that phrase, which I have heard many times, there is a good chance that they don't understand the differences between software architected for the cloud versus software architected to run on physical infrastructure in a datacenter. In their mind, it's all the same except for the location of the "datacenter." If there is no difference, why change the way we deliver software when we go to the cloud?

Value Stream Mapping

Large enterprises embark on their cloud journey with decades of baggage. They know that their legacy processes are less than ideal (for the cloud and in general), but most have never actually visualized the entire end-to-end process for building, deploying, and operating software, so they don't know how unproductive their processes really are.

This is where value stream mapping shines. Value stream mapping (VSM), as I've mentioned briefly a few times, is a pragmatic approach for visualizing all of the tasks of any process designed to create value, from beginning to end. It's a method that arose from the Lean management movement in the 1990s and has gained popularity ever since. In the software world, value is typically delivered as a service: a new capability, product, or asset. The scope of a value stream can be as simple as the help desk process for resetting a password or as complex as upgrading all laptops to the next version of Windows. For the purposes of this discussion, I will focus on value streams related to delivering infrastructure and software services.

Applying VSM best practices helps all stakeholders and participants in the process identify waste and inefficiencies in how work gets done. This is valuable information that can be used to redesign the processes to be faster and more reliable, to create better value, and to raise morale across the enterprise. In my experience, companies that don't employ process-reengineering techniques like VSM as they move to the cloud often underperform. It's hard to redesign your processes when you don't know exactly what they are.

Consultants and authors Karen Martin and Mike Osterling remind us that VSM is more than a tool; it's "a methodology to transform leadership thinking, define strategy and priorities, and assure that customers are receiving high levels of value (versus focusing merely on reducing operational waste).[2] The message here is clear: value stream mapping is an integral part of DevOps because it transforms the way our culture thinks about delivering software.

One of the main goals of VSM is to make *all* work visible. This is important because much of what we define as "waste" within the process may not be visible to all stakeholders. If nobody knows about a wasteful process, the odds of it getting optimized are slim to none. Kanban flow expert Dominica Degrandis, in her book *Making Work Visible* (IT Revolution Press), highlights five "thieves of time" that create waste in work processes: too much work in process, unknown dependencies, unplanned work, conflicting priorities, and neglected work. There's a large and long-standing body of literature on waste in work processes, with many different tools and methodologies. VSM is well suited for the software delivery process and is a popular choice among DevOps practitioners. While I am not a trained expert on the topic, I have a great deal of practical experience using it. What follows is a high-level overview to whet your appetite. There are many great books on VSM, a few of which I've quoted here, and I recommend reading at least one before jumping in.

THE VSM METHODOLOGY

Value stream mapping is a way to visually represent a process from a customer's point of view. The customer's point of view is their perception of how the overall process delivers value—and perception is reality. It's easy for a process owner to

---

2 Karen Martin and Mike Osterling, *Value Stream Mapping: How to Visualize Work and Align Leadership for Organizational Transformation* (McGraw-Hill).

design a process to satisfy their needs, but this often comes at the expense of the needs of the customer. In fact, many times the process owners are so far removed that they don't even know what the customer's experience is.

There are two ways to visualize a value stream, walking the process and holding workshops, and I recommend you use both:

Walk the process

The first is called "walking the process." I like to call it spending a day in the customer's shoes. The analyst watches the customer participate in the process throughout the day and records what they witness. There are pros and cons to this method. It can take a long time to observe enough people to come to sound conclusions, and in some cases there is observer bias, where the act of watching disrupts the flow of work. The benefit is that the eyes don't lie: you often witness steps that are invisible to the process owners.

Workshops

A value stream mapping workshop gets everyone involved in the process together to document all of the steps involved. For each step, the workshop moderators look for variations in a process, items that block the flow of work, waste, and steps that don't add value.

From this information, the analyst can document the end-to-end process and identify opportunities for improvement. Figure 4-5 shows an example of the map created during a VSM workshop.

Figure 4-6 shows a redesigned process that drastically reduces the overall lead time of the value stream.

Change management–current state

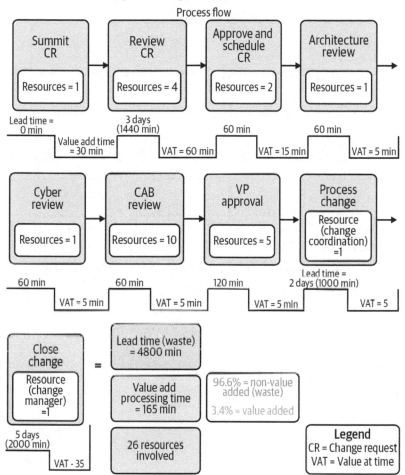

Figure 4-5. A value stream map

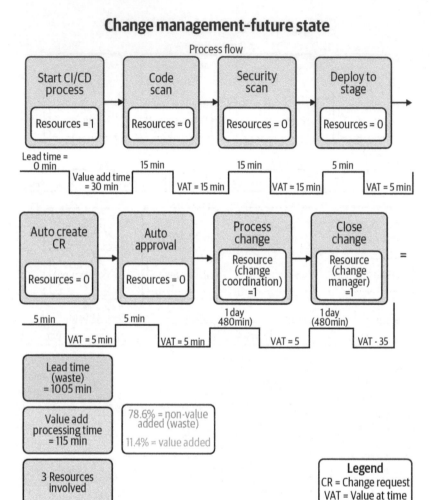

Figure 4-6. Redesigned process after the VSM workshop

HOLDING A VSM WORKSHOP

While I strongly recommend researching the VSM method yourself before beginning, I'll outline the basic steps of the process here:

Step 1: Choose your event method(s)

Decide whether you are going to hold an observation event or a workshop. In a perfect world, you would do both. The workshop is where you can collect the most information; observation can supplement that data with real-world execution of the process.

Step 2: Define your scope

Pick the scope of the process you want to map. For example, a company that's recently moved to the cloud might struggle with resolving incidents, which leads to an increase in mean time to repair. That company might want its workshop to focus on the incident management value stream.

Step 3: Plan the event

Schedule the event. This includes identifying all of the process stakeholders and finding a time where they can all participate in the workshop, in person or virtually. If key stakeholders cannot attend the event, it is better to postpone it than to risk not collecting all of the pertinent tasks and data points, which could skew your value analysis.

Step 4: Hold the VSM workshop

Perform the workshop and/or observation event. Workshops are often half-day or full-day events, depending on the size and scope of the value streams. In some cases, you might need multiple workshops to accommodate people in far flung locations, but it is highly preferred that all stakeholders participate in the same session and hear the same information at the same time.

Step 5: Validate your map

After the workshop, the analyst documents the process map and shows it to stakeholders to validate that the data was correctly captured. This can be done with another scheduled meeting with key stakeholders, in person or online.

Step 6: Analyze your map

The analyst applies the VSM methodology to the map and highlights the problem areas, such as invisible work, bottlenecks, and waste. The analyst might design the future state process in this step or schedule another workshop with stakeholders to collaborate on the new process design.

Step 7: Report your findings

The analyst reports the findings to the key stakeholders. This includes collecting all action items and identifying next steps.

Once you've completed the VSM process, you'll need to design the future state process, plan how to implement it, and execute on your plan.

I have seen VSM workshops take a month-long process down to days or even hours. It is critical to record key productivity metrics from your findings, so that once you've implemented the new process, you'll have concrete numbers to show the difference. Many workplace cultures are resistant to changing their processes. It's powerful to be able to show that the change reduced processing time by 23 days or reduced the error rate by 25% or improved the company's Net Promoter score by 10%. Factual statements like these can drive more change throughout the organization.

Conclusion: A Golden Opportunity

When incidents happen in the datacenter, no matter how good or bad the existing processes are, people know what they are and how to restore services. Even if the process is totally inefficient and requires 50 people to get on a call at 4 a.m., those teams are equipped with history, institutional knowledge, and procedural awareness.

When you move to the cloud for the first time, you are moving to a greenfield virtual datacenter. There are no processes in place. This is a one-time opportunity to design processes from the ground up, optimized for the cloud and its new ways of thinking. You'll never have a better chance to get this right. Don't simply bring your legacy processes and mindsets along for the ride. Your company's needs—all those security policies, compliance controls, and operational requirements—are still valid; it's just how you satisfy them that needs to change.

It's critical to redesign processes at all levels of the company for the cloud. To summarize, follow these guidelines as you look for opportunities for improvement:

- Focus first on the requirements or goals of the service (the "why," not the "how").

- Look for opportunities to remove waste from the existing process.

- Redesign your process with the shared responsibility model in mind.

- Automate as much as possible.

- Build trust into the system through automation and continuous monitoring.

- Move review processes from preproduction to postmortem.
- Continuously reevaluate and improve processes over time.

Process change is a key component of cloud adoption. Failing to acknowledge that legacy processes designed for another era aren't the best way to deliver software in the cloud will most likely result in low performance. This error in judgement will compound as more workloads move to the cloud, which can result in catastrophic consequences, such as risk exposure, missed SLAs, and cost overruns. Transforming a culture to be more DevOps-centric starts with good process hygiene. Pick a process pain point and optimize it for the cloud. All the technology in the world can't fix bad processes.

PART II

Cloud Operating Models: Implement Your Strategy

One of the biggest advantages of the cloud is how quickly teams can stand up infrastructure and bring new applications and services to their customers. This agility is a game-changer—but if not deployed in a secure, reliable, and compliant manner, it can also have catastrophic consequences. One of the biggest reasons that security, compliance, and infrastructure teams push back against adopting cloud is their fear that the developers will put the company at great risk because the proper controls and oversight are not in place.

You learned in Part I of this book that many of the processes and controls put in place for managing software in the datacenter do not translate well into the cloud. So how can organizations offer cloud services to their software developers while still implementing the proper controls to keep their company safe? It starts with the cloud operating model.

This chapter will introduce cloud operating models and the details of the cloud platform, including roles and platform operating models. We'll go into the differences between the various models that determine how a cloud platform operates. We'll also look at cloud governance and how to build a corporate culture that allows your platform to empower developers and other consumers.

The following chapters will continue our tour of the platform with a look at different ways to structure teams' engagement with your cloud platform, as well as the platform support models that determine how the platform manages your CSP(s).

Anatomy of an Enterprise Cloud Strategy

Before you begin designing your operating model, it is important to understand how cloud platforms fit into the overall operating model and how the overall cloud strategy and customer engagement requirements influence the organizational design. There are actually several decisions you'll need to make as you choose an operating model.

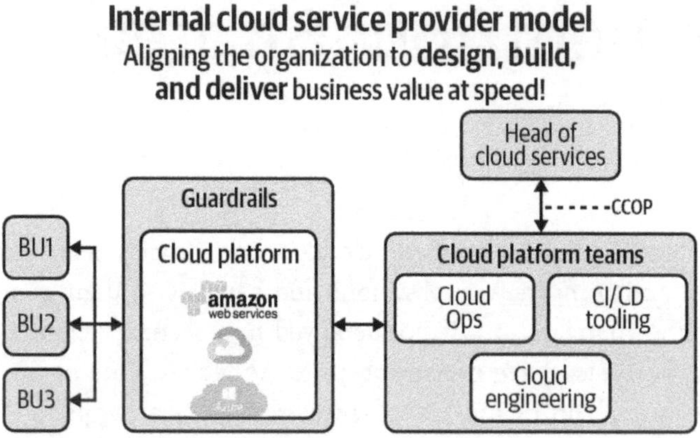

Figure 5-1. Typical cloud operating model with cloud platform

Figure 5-1 shows a typical cloud operating model. Within the operating model is the *cloud platform*. The whole thing sits inside IT. Here are the pieces we'll look at:

IT department
> An overarching factor that influences cloud platform design is the company's overall *IT operating model*. Are IT services managed by a single CIO or are there multiple CIOs per geography, business unit, or a result of a merger? The IT operating model will determine how the enterprise creates its *cloud strategy*.

Governance body
> The cloud platform is run by a governance body designed to ensure that any activity that involves cloud computing within the enterprise aligns with the overall cloud strategy. We'll discuss this body in more detail later in the chapter. The governance body's structure is determined by your *cloud operating model*.

Platform team(s)
> Beneath the governance body is the platform team (or it may be multiple teams, depending on your model; more on that in a moment). This functions as an internal cloud service provider, offering cloud services to cloud

consumers. The cloud platform team usually performs the roles of cloud engineering, operations, service desk, and sometimes pipeline management for CI/CD best practices and tool decisions.

Its structure is determined by the *cloud platform model*. Exactly how it provides those services is determined by the *engagement model* you choose. How it interacts with external cloud service providers (AWS, Google Cloud, etc.) is determined by the *platform support model* you choose.

Cloud consumers

Your cloud consumers are the internal business units, development teams, and other parts of your company that use cloud services, as well as external customers who consume APIs. The *engagement model* determines how the platform team interacts with consumers.

The roles of the platform team are easy to grasp, but to understand the scope of what the platform is responsible for, you must take a lot into consideration. The *cloud strategy* determines which cloud platforms the company is going to support. *Consumer engagement requirements*, or the needs of consumers, drive cloud platform design decisions as well. A good cloud platform customizes its engagement to meet the needs of its customers: that's the *engagement model*, which I'll introduce later in this chapter.

These factors influence the design and the scope of the cloud platform teams. In the next two chapters, we'll look at them all.

Understanding Cloud Operating Models

Before we get into some of the common cloud operating models, it is important to differentiate between an IT operating model and a cloud operating model.

An *IT operating model* is a visual representation of how an organization delivers value from all of IT's capabilities to its customers.

A *cloud operating model* is a visual representation of how an organization delivers value from cloud services to its customers. It is a subset of the overall IT operating model. This chapter will focus only on the cloud operating model, not how it plugs into the overall IT operating model. (That could be a whole other book.)

Cloud operating models fall into three main categories: *centralized, decentralized,* and *federated.* There are pros and cons to each model, and which works best for an organization will be influenced by many factors.

Operating models change based on how much of your organization falls within the scope of the cloud strategy. These changes can take place at the enterprise level, a regional or geographical level (including global), or a local level (such as a business unit or functional team). In fact, most successful cloud initiatives start small, at a local level, and expand as the cloud program matures. Your operating model should change incrementally as it is implemented at each of these levels.

Here are some common factors that drive operating model design:

The people driving the change

Is the change coming from the top down, coming up from the grassroots, or both? If it's coming from the top and its advocates have a great deal of clout in the organization, it's more likely operating model changes can be designed at the enterprise or regional level. If the change is a grassroots effort, any operating model changes will probably only take place at the local level.

Organizational characteristics

The size and complexity of the organization has a substantial impact on the operating model design. Is the organization global or based in just one country? Does it focus mainly on one core product or service, or is it a conglomerate offering many different unrelated services? Are the employees geographically concentrated or highly distributed?

Organizational culture

Is the organization tech-savvy? Does it embrace or resist change? Is the industry highly regulated, favoring control over agility, or does industry culture believe in empowering business units (BUs)? Is the organization's workforce mostly outsourced or in house? All of these factors influence the design of its cloud operating model.

Cloud maturity

Where an organization is in its cloud journey is a huge factor in operating model design. If the change is starting with a single team or BU, there is less of a need for a major overhaul of the current operating model. As organizations get more mature in the cloud, they come to see the negative effect of their legacy operating model on building and deploying services in the cloud. Once they gain that understanding, they can make more significant changes to the operating model.

Cloud strategy

Is the organization's strategy to adopt cloud globally? Is the organization going all-in on one cloud provider, or using a multicloud or hybrid cloud strategy (or both)? (I'll discuss all of these later in the chapter.) Does it plan to outsource cloud operations to a managed service provider (MSP)? Your organization's overall cloud strategy will drastically change the design of its cloud operating model.

With these factors in mind, let's take a look at the most common kinds of cloud operating models.

Operating Model Archetypes

There are three common models that enterprises typically embrace: centralized, decentralized, and federated (see Figure 5-2).

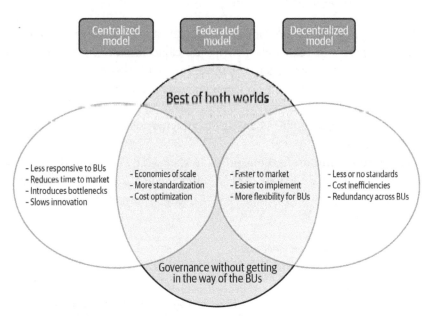

Figure 5-2. The three archetypes most cloud operating models follow

Let's look at each one in detail.

CENTRALIZED MODEL

Often known as "command and control," the *centralized cloud operating model* (Figure 5-3) grants ownership of all core functions and resources to a single department or organization, which takes full responsibility for the end-to-end delivery of all cloud services to customers across the enterprise. About 80% of enterprises in the cloud use this model.

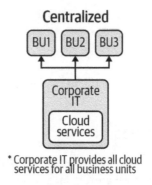

Figure 5-3. Centralized cloud operating model

This is the most common model in companies where the datacenter, infrastructure, or operations teams are driving the cloud initiative. It's often seen in highly regulated industries, where organizations don't feel safe in adopting the cloud; out of caution, they often prioritize security and compliance over speed to market and developer productivity. While loosening the level of centralization can ease these issues, it can be a hard sell to an enterprise taking its first tentative steps into the cloud.

It is also very common for enterprises to start with a centralized model early in their cloud journey, and then shift to other models later, when they reach a certain level of maturity and compliance. Table 5-1 shows some of the pros and cons of this model.

Table 5-1. Centralized model pros and cons

Advantages	Disadvantages
Drives standardization and consistency	Process bottlenecks can make the system slower and less responsive to customer needs
Easier to manage	Can reduce developer agility and preferences
Better security and compliance	Often restrictive, longer lead times for access
Economy of scale reduces tool and resource sprawl	Offers customers less flexibility
Greater comfort level for enterprises with low cloud maturity	Can slow down customers who are highly mature in the cloud

It's not uncommon for an infrastructure or security team to implement the command-and-control model with little to no feedback from the development teams. The result is usually a bad user experience for developers—which can, as you learned in Chapter 1, increase the amount of "shadow IT" that goes unmanaged within the organization. When implementing this model, make sure you consider the usability of your cloud services so developers can be productive. If the services are cumbersome to use or there are too many steps to navigate through to consume the services, they will go elsewhere to meet their needs.

A fintech company I'll call Carlow Financial decided to pivot to public cloud because it was not getting the value it desired out of its private cloud implementation. Carlow's corporate culture was ultraconservative and based on command and control. It prioritized security and compliance over agility, even though the business units were screaming for improved speed to market. The centralized model was an easy choice, being a model the infrastructure, security, and governance teams were very familiar with. The developers were excited about starting the cloud journey because they expected to be able to deliver much faster, without all of the physical infrastructure.

The results were mixed. What worked well was that the developers could leverage a secure and compliant cloud platform that came with robust security, monitoring, and logging frameworks. They didn't have to focus on infrastructure or manage any of the tools associated with it. Even the CI/CD toolchain was managed for them.

The downside was that they were still just as highly dependent on the operations and infrastructure teams as ever. They also had little input into the technology choices, which were made by the central team. This was a huge source of frustration for the developers, especially around the CI/CD tooling. The guardrails implemented did not consider the developers' productivity, only the needs of the security and governance teams.

In short, there was still a great divide between silos, especially between dev and ops and between dev and security. While the centralized operating model benefited Carlow from a security and governance standpoint, it did not allow the developers to get products to market much faster than before.

In the centralized model, everything is run from a core IT group: the cloud platform team. The cloud operations team is a subset of the platform team. (We'll look more closely at the platform team later in this chapter.) In this model, the BUs are writing apps on top of the cloud platform. The cloud platform team operates the cloud platform, not the apps. Tool selection, user access, vendor management, patching, monitoring, logging, and so forth must all go through the platform team. They manage accounts for all groups. They have a great deal of control over compliance and security, especially with regard to what goes into production. Because everyone uses common tools, the centralized model makes it easier to work in a more standard manner; however, this lack of variety can make the cloud platform too prescriptive and it might not provide the options that the developers prefer and need.

Running everything centrally can be slow. When everyone depends on one team, that team can easily become a bottleneck.

DECENTRALIZED MODEL

The *decentralized cloud operating model* (Figure 5-4) empowers departments or BUs to manage core functions and services for themselves. In this model, the cloud platform team serves as a "center of excellence" that informs and advises, researches, and provides guidance to each group, which then makes its own decisions. About 10% of enterprises in the cloud use a decentralized cloud operating model.

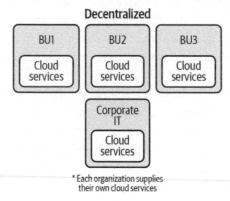

Figure 5-4. Decentralized cloud operating model

This model is often seen in highly distributed companies, where each department or country has its own IT leadership and staff. It's also common when a large company acquires a smaller one that already has an established cloud program. Grassroots-driven cloud initiatives often result in decentralized models.

In a decentralized model, each department or BU owns responsibility not only for the application layer but for the infrastructure layer as well. All of the functions performed by the cloud platform team in the centralized model become the responsibility of *each* BU. The good news is that the BUs can move much faster, because they are in total control of their cloud solutions; the downside is that they can end up reinventing the wheel and will most likely each implement the infrastructure layer with different tools and processes.

Cloud maturity has an important role here. If each BU is already experienced and mature in the cloud, a centralized team could slow them down substantially. If your customers are already self-sufficient, there's no need to disrupt what they're doing.

Like the other models, it too has its advantages and disadvantages (see Table 5-2).

Table 5-2. Decentralized model pros and cons

Advantages	Disadvantages
Greater agility	Often leads to redundant efforts across departments; less economy of scale
Teams are more self-sufficient	Less knowledge sharing across the organization
More responsive to customer needs	Increased risk of security and compliance issues
Quicker access to CSPs' new cloud service offerings	Patchworked use of resources and tools

An eCommerce company I'll call Carnegie Fashion acquired numerous online startups over the years. These startups were born in the cloud and built their solutions from the ground up in true cloud native fashion, and had strong track records of extreme agility and responsiveness to customer needs. Each acquired startup became a standalone business unit. The one thing Carnegie wanted to ensure was that the transition didn't affect that agility and responsiveness. Carnegie also knew how slow its corporate IT was, and that there was a lack of cloud knowledge internally. The new business units, on the other hand, had some of the top cloud talent in the industry. The company decided to implement a decentralized cloud platform model.

The decentralized model had its trade-offs. The new acquisitions paid off well, because these cloud-savvy teams were still bringing new features to the market regularly and continued to drive new revenue to the bottom line. But each business unit had its own preferences in tools and processes, and different levels of sophistication when it came to implementing best-of-breed security practices. A couple of the BUs had very poor security hygiene that put the parent company at risk. Carnegie made efforts to educate these BUs and improve their security hygiene, but they prioritized agility and customer satisfaction over security (as opposed to Carlow Financial).

Decentralized cloud operations models are often a good fit for companies that are deploying software multiple times a day, and value agility and speed to market over security and compliance. When different business units are permitted to choose their own tools without central control, developers get what they want—but the resulting patchwork of tools can allow gaps in compliance and security. Thus, decentralization is a better fit for companies that are not in highly regulated industries, have highly mature business units, or have a business unit that is the first team to embark on the cloud journey.

FEDERATED MODEL

Sometimes known as a mixed model, the *federated model* (Figure 5-5) centralizes a set of core functions and resources within a single department or organization, and allows the BUs to manage noncore services and resources.

In this model, the core team functions like an internal cloud service provider; their job is to provide core cloud infrastructure as a service to their internal customers (the BUs). (I'll discuss this more in Chapter 6.)

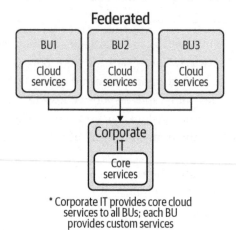

Figure 5-5. Federated cloud operating model

The federated model is often seen in organizations that have business units that already have cloud skills but still want to maintain a level of control in order to optimize spending and mitigate security and compliance risks. Treating everyone the same doesn't work when different business units are at different levels of cloud maturity. You might even have situations where some BUs have higher cloud maturity than the cloud platform team!

In such cases, the federated model lets those experienced BUs leverage only the platform services they want and develop the services they desire on top of the platform. It enables them to consume the services that meet their needs and refrain from using the services that don't. They're free to build or manage their own infrastructure or relinquish control to the CSP, and can ask for help as they need it.

It's the best of both worlds: those teams that are self-sufficient and cloud-savvy can take on more responsibility and are free to do so, while less cloud-mature units can turn to the platform team for help. There's room for different parts of the enterprise to move at different paces that make sense for them, and the enterprise still maintains enough control to ensure compliance. Developers don't have to wait on the platform teams to build everything for them. If there is a gap in the capabilities that the platform provides, they can fill it themselves without waiting. If the platform introduces the capability later, the development team can migrate to that platform service if it meets their needs. In this model, core IT relinquishes some control in return for developer agility. The art to this is determining which services to maintain as core capabilities and which to delegate to the business units.

Let's fast-forward now to see how things turned out for our ecommerce company. Over the next two years of its cloud journey, Carnegie started acquiring strong cloud talent in its core business by both hiring cloud talent and training its existing talent. The Carnegie developers had a different set of constraints than those in the acquired business units. Although they were building new cloud native applications, the bulk of their work involved migrating legacy applications and working with complex hybrid architectures. This brought many additional security controls and governance policies into scope. At the same time, there were a few security vulnerabilities that did not get patched effectively in all of the business units.

Carnegie decided it was finally time to move away from the decentralized model and into a federated model. It still wanted to be sensitive to the business units' needs, but not at the expense of major security risks and cost inefficiencies. So Carnegie selected a few services that it would manage centrally and mandated their use across the entire company. The first thing Carnegie took over was managing the operating systems. It set up a system in which it provided a repository of approved operating systems images, with the appropriate controls in place. The business units now had to change their CI/CD process to get the latest operating system image from this repository. This improved the patching process, because the central team could patch the operating system image and make it available for all other teams.

Carnegie also decided to pull the CI/CD tooling into the core platform team, because it was paying so many vendors for the same functionality (eight different logging solutions, for example). Carnegie decided to standardize on the top three tools in each category; so the developers would still have some flexibility. The platform team also beefed up their service catalog to support the additional use cases that enterprise IT had to contend with, but did not force the other business units to adhere to those new services and processes.

The federated model is common when there is a lot of diversity in both the cloud maturity of the business units and the risk profiles and complexities of the products and services they are delivering to their customers.

Cloud Platform Roles

Regardless of which operating model an organization chooses, I recommend assigning a team to building a cloud platform.

A *cloud platform*, as discussed briefly in Chapter 3, provides a core set of enterprise-class cloud services to be consumed by the various development teams. Many companies build their own internal cloud platforms to meet their specific needs; some use third-party platforms from PaaS providers; still others prefer to outsource their platform needs to a managed-services provider. It is also not uncommon for a company to use more than one cloud platform. For example, many companies provide an internal cloud platform that includes a PaaS solution as part of its service catalog in addition to its IaaS services. In the decentralized model, some business units may choose to leverage a managed service provider, while others build their own platforms.

Figure 5-6 is a logical representation of what a cloud platform operating model should look like.

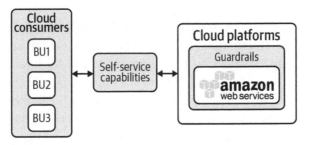

Figure 5-6. A cloud platform operating model

You can see that the cloud platform team provides a service catalog, with some level of self-service capabilities, to the cloud consumers (typically BUs). The platform team is responsible for applying all relevant security policies and regulatory controls on top of what's provided by the CSP or CSPs (in this example, AWS), so that the cloud consumers can build software in a safe and monitored environment.

The cloud platform team is an internal CSP and should organize and operate with the mindset that it is creating a product. The product is the platform; the value created is offering secure, compliant, and auditable cloud services approved by the GRC teams (which was discussed in Chapter 1).

The cloud platform includes a variety of roles, as shown in Figure 5-7. Some of these roles might be filled by individuals, others by dedicated teams or teams that perform multiple roles.

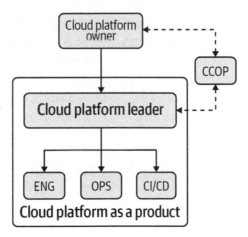

Figure 5-7. Cloud platform roles

Cloud platform owner

The cloud platform team should be owned, either directly or indirectly, by a very senior executive who also either owns or greatly influences the overall cloud strategy. Usually they are at least at the director level, but most often they are a VP or even a CTO. The platform owner should think and act like a CSP and create a product-driven culture within the platform team. Their goals should be empowering the cloud consumers, facilitating developer agility, and keeping users safe by providing secure and compliant services.

Underneath this executive is the cloud platform team, led by a senior leader within IT.

Cloud platform leader

The *cloud platform leader*, should have significant experience with cloud computing (and not solely from an infrastructure standpoint). Since the product is the platform and the customers are the developers, they should also have both infrastructure and application experience, or a great track record of being an advocate of development and the other cloud consumers.

The cloud platform leader is responsible for both building and running the platform: you build it, you run it.

Governance

Cloud governance is another important role within the cloud platform. The governance function provides oversight for all cloud activity. Governance is crucial because, without a secure, compliant enterprise-class cloud platform, an organization can be exposed to huge risks. These can include security breaches, compliance fines, cost overruns, unmet customer SLAs, and many other unwanted scenarios that will put the organization in the news for all the wrong reasons. Each enterprise defines the scope of its governance role and determines how passive or assertive its enforcement policies will be. We'll look more closely at this body in a moment.

The cloud platform organization itself is usually made up of three distinct roles: cloud engineering, cloud operations, and cloud delivery automation, usually referred to as CI/CD:

Cloud engineering

The cloud engineering role is responsible for building all the automation scripts to provision the necessary infrastructure. This includes logging, monitoring and security frameworks, infrastructure blueprints, and much more.

Cloud operations

Cloud operations (CloudOps) is the role for managing and monitoring the uptime and performance of the platform. CloudOps also provides platform support for the cloud consumers. A key point here is that CloudOps should not own the operations of the cloud applications. Instead they only own the operations of the *platform*, just as AWS, Azure, and GCP are responsible for their services, not your apps.

Cloud delivery automation (CI/CD)

The third role focuses around the tooling and processes for automating the build and deployment pipeline, commonly referred to as CI/CD (or, dreadfully, labelled as "the DevOps team"). In some enterprises CI/CD is centrally owned by the platform team. In others, the CI/CD role focuses more on being a center of excellence and working with the cloud consumers to ensure their pipelines are secure and compliant and follow best practices. Some organizations have the luxury of mandating which tools or pipelines consumers can use, but that is rare. In large enterprises, it is highly likely that business units already have their desired pipeline tools, so the CI/CD team acts more as evangelists and trainers for building pipelines.

The cloud platform team is, in essence, an internal cloud service provider. Developers go to the platform, not directly to the CSPs, to consume cloud services. This allows the company to control what services are consumed and how. You can see in Figure 5-6 that the cloud platform team builds "guardrails" around the cloud services and makes them available to the BUs. The CloudOps team is responsible for ensuring that the platform's SLAs are met.

Your organization's cloud strategy will drive a lot of the operating model decisions for your cloud platform. Some of the decision points that influence the model design are:

- What cloud service models will the platform support (IaaS, PaaS, SaaS)?

- Where will the customers reside (local, regional, global)?

- What is the cloud architecture strategy (all-in single cloud, multicloud, hybrid, cloud agnostic)?

- Who will manage it (IT, BU, outsourced)?

Before you begin designing the operating model for your cloud platform, though, I want to make you aware of what to do—and, more importantly, what not to do—when implementing a cloud platform.

So that they're right at the front of your mind, let's review the main goals of a cloud platform:

- Implement and enforce security standards

- Implement and enforce compliance policies

- Control which cloud services are allowed to be consumed

- Contain and monitor costs of cloud services consumption

- Centralize access to cloud services

- Ensure cloud consumption aligns with the overall cloud strategy

- Provide self-service capabilities to cloud consumers

- Provide standard tooling and prevent cloud-vendor tooling sprawl

- Manage cloud-vendor relationships, including contract negotiation

Now that you have a feel for the basic shape of the platform and its roles, let's look more closely at the top of the platform: the governance body.

Governance and the Cloud Community of Practice

Every cloud operating model should include a governance body, often called the *cloud business office* (CBO) or *cloud center of excellence* (CCOE). I call it the *cloud community of practice* (CCOP)—more on that in a moment. Not to be confused with a security or compliance organization, this group's main mission is to ensure that any activity that involves cloud computing within the enterprise aligns with the overall cloud strategy.

Its responsibilities include providing financial oversight and cost control guidance, and establishing processes for permitting and onboarding new cloud services and third-party vendor solutions. The cloud governance body is also responsible for making sure that:

- All cloud activity directionally aligns with the cloud strategy
- All activity meets the necessary security, risk, and controls requirements
- Training and educational services are available
- Key metrics are measured and reported on

Each enterprise will have its own list of responsibilities, but these are the top ones I recommend. Adding too much responsibility can make this group a huge bottleneck.

Also, note that owning the *responsibility* for a function does not mean the CCOP *executes* the tasks involved with that function. For example, the CCOP is highly unlikely to actually manage vendor contracts and negotiations, but it is responsible for ensuring that those who *do* manage them do so in a way that aligns with the overall cloud strategy.

A word about nomenclature: the terms CBO and center of excellence (COE) can have negative connotations in some enterprises, particularly if there's a history of heavy-handed governance. I have seen enterprises give their governing bodies more creative names, like "Nerve Center" or "Cloud Strategy Office."

I personally prefer *cloud community of practice* (CCOP) for a couple of reasons. The CCOP is more than just another name for a governance team: it is a mindset for how different groups can work together toward a common goal. Communities of practice are groups of people who share a concern, a set of problems, or a passion about a topic, and who deepen their knowledge and expertise in this area by interacting on an ongoing basis.

I recommend finding a name that does not give the group a negative image; but what is most important to communicate is what this group is responsible for and how they execute their duties in a way that does not diminish the agility value of cloud computing.

The CCOP drives the enterprise's cloud strategy throughout the organization as it adopts cloud computing at scale. Where the CCOP sits within the organization depends on two major, and related, factors: the company's culture and its approach to the cloud platform. Let's discuss these.

PLATFORM CULTURE

In a perfect world, everyone at a company embarking on its cloud journey would understand that building and running software and services in the cloud is radically different than running traditional software in traditional datacenters. They wouldn't constrain themselves with legacy organizational structures and ideologies when designing organizational structures and processes for the cloud.

But this isn't a perfect world, and too often, the people or teams that have always owned governance in their silos insist on doing the same in the cloud. This usually results in a CCOP that is owned and operated by people who aren't very knowledgeable about cloud computing and aren't willing to reinvent their legacy processes and mindset.

The preventative approach

Often, infrastructure teams build guardrails and access controls for cloud, but not as a product. Instead, the CCOP is simply a silo, often named "DevOps," with its own set of priorities that usually align more with those of the VP of infrastructure than those of the cloud strategy and the BUs. Instead of building platform services to enable developer agility, "DevOps" silos often become a new bottleneck in the software development process. Don't get me wrong: they can also deliver a ton of value by automating and creating standard infrastructure images, providing security and monitoring frameworks, managing access, and much more. But when the mission is not focused on the developers, the processes for leveraging the cloud platform mirror those designed for physical infrastructure in the datacenter.

When this is the case, the CCOP is often owned by the infrastructure organization and becomes more like a project management office. The processes are designed to make sure "devs don't do stupid stuff" rather than designed to drive agility safely. The CCOP simply becomes a new silo (as shown in Figure 5-8). It becomes a new way to say "NO!" to everything cloud related.

Unfortunately, many cloud initiatives have no choice but to start their CCOP in this manner. Their organizations need time to learn about and embrace the cloud before they think about governance in a new light.

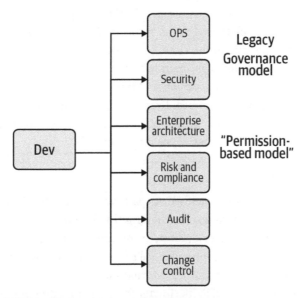

Figure 5-8. The CCOP in a legacy-driven organization

The empowering approach

The CCOP works best in corporate cultures that are willing to transform themselves because they understand the cloud requires a new way of working.

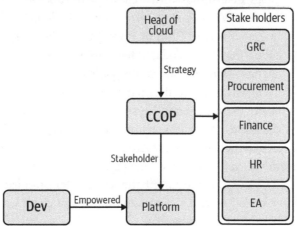

Figure 5-9. The CCOP as traveling partner in the cloud journey

Such organizations usually create the CCOP as a group that owns the cloud strategy *and* the cloud platform, as pictured in Figure 5-9. In this model, the CCOP is a traveling partner in the cloud journey, not a roadblock.

When the cloud platform is operated as a product, the CCOP focuses on what I like to call *frictionless governance*. Many of its controls and policies are driven through the platform services. Processes for requesting things like access, new service-catalog items, onboarding, training, etc. are optimized through automation, self-service, and workflow as much as possible.

Platform Models

Before designing your cloud platform organizational model, it is important to understand all the factors that go into making this key decision.

As you've seen, the typical cloud operating model encompasses a governance body (CCOP), a cloud service provider (platform teams), and cloud consumers (business units, development teams, external customers consuming APIs, etc.). The cloud platform team usually performs the roles of cloud engineering, cloud operations, cloud service desk, and sometimes cloud pipeline management for CI/CD best practices and tool decisions.

Sounds simple, right? Well, it's not that easy. The roles of the platform team are easy to grasp, but the scope of what the platform is responsible for must take a lot into consideration. Two major factors that influence the platform team's scope are the cloud strategy and the customer engagement requirements.

The cloud strategy determines which cloud platforms the company is going to support. Are they an AWS-only shop? Are they multicloud? Hybrid? Will they be using PaaS solutions like OpenShift or Pivotal Cloud Foundry? These are just some of the decisions that the cloud strategy drives. We'll discuss this aspect more in the next chapter, when we talk about platform support models.

The customer engagement requirements drive cloud platform design decisions as well. Will the platform team be servicing all cloud consumers for the company? What categories of cloud consumers will they be servicing? Are they internal customers, external customers? Are they cloud-savvy or can't spell cloud? A good cloud platform customizes its engagement to meet the needs of its customers. Not all customers need or want the same level of engagement. Cloud-savvy customers want self-service. Customers new to the cloud want more white-glove service (more on that in Chapter 6).

Another factor that influences cloud platform design is the overall IT operating model. Are IT services managed by a single CIO or are there multiple CIOs per geography, business unit, or as a result of a merger?

All of these factors influence the design and the scope of the cloud platform teams.

There are three models typically implemented for cloud platforms: single, distributed, and hybrid.

SINGLE-PLATFORM MODEL

Perhaps the most common pattern is to implement a single cloud platform, or a centralized model (echoing, and often overlapping with, the centralized cloud operating model). I call this the *single-platform model*. It is purpose-built to be a single standard for the entire enterprise.

In this model, a single cloud platform team supports all cloud consumers across the enterprise, regardless of geographic location. The platform team also supports all cloud endpoints, including hybrid and multicloud implementations, as shown in Figure 5-10.

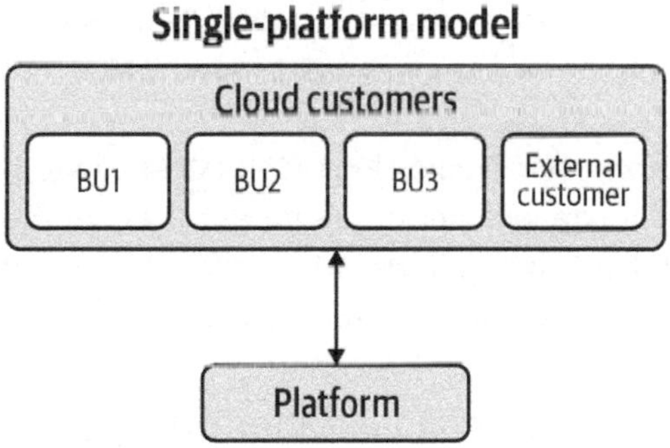

Single-platform model

Figure 5-10. The single-platform model

The advantages of the single-platform model are many and include common standards, policies, and guardrails that apply across all cloud workloads. Cloud services are used consistently across the organization. Cloud vendor tools and services are rationalized to prevent tool sprawl and deliver a consistent service catalog across the organization. The organization's leaders get a single view into their cloud metrics, so they can easily chart progress toward the enterprise's cloud strategy goals. There's more control of security and compliance activities, which become easier to audit. It's also easier to manage and visualize cloud costs.

There are also trade-offs. For instance, prioritizing the backlog could be a bottleneck for BUs or geographies that are not top revenue or risk targets. Trying to service all cloud endpoints from a single common set of tools can sometimes create unwarranted complexity. Furthermore, if the CCOP doesn't use different engagement models for different customers (as described in Chapter 6), the platform could be too targeted to novice or high-risk cloud consumers and fail to meet the needs of cloud-savvy and highly agile teams.

DISTRIBUTED PLATFORM MODEL

In some large enterprises, certain BUs can build and run their own cloud platforms. You saw some examples of this earlier in the chapter when we discussed decentralized operating models. A common use case here is an enterprise that acquires a new company, complete with its own cloud platform. Large conglomerates that contain many different business functions with different business models often have their own IT organizations that run independently of each other. In such cases, each different business function is responsible for its own platform. This platform model, called the *distributed platform model*, maps closely to the decentralized cloud operating model.

Some enterprises choose to build separate platforms for each CSP they use. For instance, a company might create an on-prem cloud platform for private cloud, and a public cloud platform for any public cloud CSPs. In fact, we have often seen one platform per public cloud CSP. Most of the time, the "one platform per CSP" model happens not by design but through the evolution of separate grassroots cloud initiative efforts, with little to no collaboration or shared knowledge. Figure 5-11 shows how this often looks.

Distributed platform model

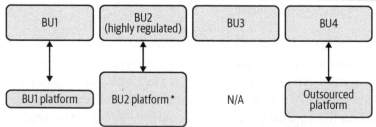

*Larger size depicts larger amount of controls implemented

Figure 5-11. The distributed platform model

The advantages of this pattern include making it easier to customize the platform for specific needs. Cloud tool and vendor selections, too, can be more specialized, allowing cloud consumers to choose the tools they favor. Platform owners have their own budget and backlogs. These tend to be more focused on BU goals than on the goals of the entire organization, which allows for more customization, better agility, easier prioritization, and less complexity.

This model also allows a measure of independence from the big machine called "corporate," which tends to move at a much slower pace.

The disadvantages, however, may be more than leadership can tolerate. They include the possibility of "reinventing the wheel," and a sprawl of tools across the organization as each platform purchases its own tools and solves its own problems. Smaller platforms mean less leverage to negotiate vendor contracts. In addition, it can be harder to standardize, govern, secure, audit, and control cloud costs.

Distributed platforms may make more sense for different geographies or business units if they each have their own CIO and CTO, or if they have independent business models with completely different risk models.

HYBRID PLATFORM MODEL

It is also possible to combine multiple patterns. Most enterprises have a centralized enterprise cloud platform, even if other BUs or geographies implement their own cloud platforms. This is a *hybrid platform model*. In this model, the enterprise is the default platform for all workloads. Any BU that does not have the skills, resources, or desire to run its own cloud platform can leverage the centralized pattern. Certain business units or geographies with permission to build their own cloud platforms may take on the cloud platform responsibilities (shown in Figure 5-12). This model is common in companies with a federated cloud operating model.

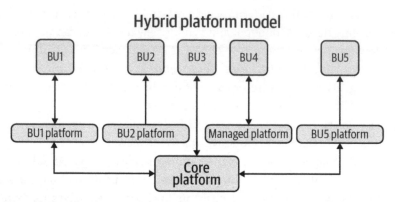

Figure 5-12. The hybrid platform model

Even when other cloud platforms exist, you can still choose to centralize some cloud services within the enterprise platform. For example, some companies centralize the creation and cataloging of all operating-system blueprints and patching.

Unfortunately, in many cases it is not the cloud strategy that drives these decisions. Hybrid models can arise for all of the wrong reasons. Lack of collaboration/communication can be a big factor: multiple teams might be building platforms without realizing that similar efforts are happening elsewhere in the organization. Empire building is a concern, too: sometimes leaders want control of cloud platforms and cloud resources for the sake of their own career aspirations, rather than because it's best for the company. Another important factor is the lack of trust, as discussed in detail in Chapter 1: because corporate IT departments often have a terrible track record of delivery and treat the cloud like a datacenter, the BUs abandon that platform and roll their own.

Conclusion

Now that you're familiar with the basic components of the cloud platform and the most important types of cloud operating models and platform models, let's move into Chapter 6, where we'll discuss two more models that shape the cloud platform: consumer engagement models and platform support models.

6

Platform Engagement and Support Models

In Chapter 5, you learned about the cloud operating model, the overarching structure that shapes how the enterprise works in the cloud. We looked at the roles of the cloud platform, its governance, and the models that structure it. You also learned briefly about two more kinds of models: consumer engagement models, which govern how the platform provides cloud services to various types of consumers, and platform support models, which govern how the platform manages its public and/or private cloud service providers. In this chapter I'll dive into the details of those two types of models. We'll finish our tour of the platform with some antipatterns to avoid and best practices to implement, as well as some advice for making the right decisions for your enterprise's platform.

Engagement Models

I recommend creating categories of customers and providing a different engagement model for each so they can all be serviced in a way that maximizes their customer experience. This section will guide you through the four basic engagement models, shown in Table 6-1.

Table 6-1. Levels of customer cloud knowledge and appropriate engagement models

Customer type	Cloud knowledge	Engagement model
Beginner	Little to no experience with cloud technology; may not be comfortable with technology in general	White-glove service
Intermediate	Some basic cloud knowledge; has a general sense of what the cloud is and how it works, but no advanced or specialized knowledge	DevOps as a service

Customer type	Cloud knowledge	Engagement model
Experienced	Deep experience with cloud technology; knowledgeable about DevOps, CI/CD, etc.; has specialized knowledge	NoOps/self-service
Outsourced	Not experienced with cloud, but working with third-party partners with expert knowledge	Managed

WHITE-GLOVE SERVICE

Some BUs or business owners of a software product may have little or no cloud computing skills or resources. They rely heavily on the cloud platform team to provide most of their IT services.

Every quarter, the vendor issues updates that the finance team must vet before the software is deployed into production. No one on the finance team is skilled in cloud infrastructure, so they need the platform team to provision a test environment and update. Imagine that a finance team purchases a market analytics tool that is deployed on the company's primary cloud provider's infrastructure. The finance team performs the validation, then asks the platform team to coordinate and execute the upgrade.

White-glove service is not just for business users, though. If a team is onboarded to the cloud platform very early in its cloud journey, the members of that team may require a lot of hand-holding before they can take advantage of the platform's self-service capabilities. In fact, some heavily regulated enterprises require *all* teams to start with the white-glove service engagement model until they prove that they have the rigor, skills, and capabilities to move to another engagement model.

DEVOPS AS A SERVICE

In this engagement model, the platform provides all of the tooling required to provision infrastructure and build and deploy software. BUs are presented with a service catalog consisting of infrastructure blueprints and the necessary scripts to integrate the underlying logging, monitoring, and security frameworks and tooling with the infrastructure.

Often, a standard CI/CD toolchain is provided and sometimes even mandated. The platform team sets the standards for all processes and tooling to prevent BUs from buying their own tools and reinventing the wheel.

This is the most common engagement model for highly regulated enterprises and those used to a centralized command-and-control model.

NO OPS

NoOps is a misunderstood term. It does not mean that there are no operational responsibilities or no operators. We use NoOps to describe developers' desire to consume services that abstract away the underlying infrastructure, without the need to submit a ticket to provision infrastructure on the developer's behalf. I like to call it "less ops" to make it less controversial.

The NoOps engagement model is how cloud service providers engage with their customers. Go to AWS, Azure, or GCP's web control panel and you will see a large number of services for you to leverage to build whatever product or service you desire. The CSPs are not involved in any way with how and when you use their services. They are available to provide guidance if you need it, but you can leverage their service catalog any way you wish.

Enterprises can also engage this way with their customers, the BUs. In this model, the platform team provides any support and guidance that the BUs request, but is not needed to provision any infrastructure for them. The BUs self-provision infrastructure from the platform team's service catalog. If the platform does not offer the required services or if a service does not meet their needs or preferences, the BUs can install and manage the necessary service.

This model is common when the BU is very experienced and mature in the cloud. Enterprises that acquire cloud native companies are likely to engage in this manner with the acquired company. The acquired company may already have implemented its own CI/CD pipeline, with different tooling than the platform team's standard. The platform team may also be behind in its maturity and lack capabilities that the acquired company requires.

In some enterprises, the cloud journey starts with building out a platform team. In many others, the cloud journey starts with a product team or with the company's .com website. Only after a number of cloud projects are implemented does the leadership start to implement the cloud platform team. When this happens, some BUs are well ahead of the platform team, much like a born-in-the-cloud startup that has been acquired. The DevOps as a service or white-glove service models would actually be detrimental to such a BU.

MANAGED

In the managed services engagement model, all of the cloud infrastructure is outsourced to a third-party provider that is responsible for fully managing, operating, and supporting it. This model is often very rigidly defined by the contract between the two parties. Many managed service providers (MSPs) come from traditional hosting backgrounds and (unfortunately) provide a similar experience to their customers.

For smaller companies without large IT budgets, though, managed services can be a good way to go. Even large companies leverage this model when they want to accelerate getting into the cloud without having to retrain and upskill their staff up front. The managed service model allows them to make use of the vendor's capabilities while they ramp up their capabilities over time. Some companies simply want to get out of the infrastructure business altogether and are happy to pay a third party to manage it all.

MSPs have their own engagement models for interacting with their customers; "your mileage may vary" by vendor, so choose wisely.

Platform Support Models

A platform support model should align with the overall cloud strategy. Does the enterprise want to go "all in" with a single public cloud provider? Is it leveraging multiple cloud providers? Is it leveraging both private (on-prem) and public cloud services? Will it run all compute (cloud and noncloud) from one team, or look to a two-speed IT model with separate models for legacy workloads and cloud workloads? Here are four common platform support models.

SINGLE CLOUD MODEL ("ALL IN")

When an enterprise goes "all in" with a single cloud provider, it typically values speed to market over the risk of vendor lock-in. This allows the enterprise to leverage the full service catalog of its chosen CSP. This creates tremendous advantages for the developers because they focus more on the application layer to address their business requirements, and leave the infrastructure and middleware layers to the CSPs.

MULTICLOUD MODEL

Many companies that leverage the public cloud use more than one CSP. A 2019 Gartner survey (*https://oreil.ly/F5-ar*) found that 81% of respondents claimed they were working with 2 or more public cloud providers. Many people interpret this as 81% of companies have a multicloud strategy, but just because companies have more than one public cloud doesn't mean it's a strategy. Sometimes multicloud is a strategy, but many times it happens because there are many cloud projects happening ungoverned throughout an enterprise.

There are two different approaches for strategically choosing a multicloud strategy: you can reduce vendor lock-in with a *cloud agnostic* approach, or leverage different clouds for best-in-breed services, known as the *best cloud for the job* approach.

Cloud agnostic

It's very common for the cloud agnostic approach to be driven by risk management and security teams. The reason to require software to be cloud agnostic is so that the enterprise can limit the amount of lock-in to a single cloud provider. When enterprises choose to be cloud agnostic, they are treating the public cloud as a commoditized IaaS (infrastructure as a service) layer and disallow the use of most proprietary services that the CSPs provide.

This adds much more work to the platform teams because now the platform needs to provide much of the capabilities that existed with the proprietary services of the CSP. For example, AWS, Azure, and GCP all have a managed Kubernetes service which automatically provisions, scales, and manages container clusters. Since proprietary APIs are not allowed in the cloud agnostic strategy, platform teams must provide that functionality by installing and managing their own Kubernetes clusters, or they may choose to leverage a PaaS provider like Red Hat OpenShift or Pivotal Cloud Foundry as their container management strategy.

The same applies to all other proprietary services. All of the cloud vendors have managed services in the areas of machine learning, event streaming, big data services, and IoT services, to name a few. Platform teams will have to build or buy solutions to include in their platform.

Best cloud for the job

Some enterprises use multiple clouds because they prefer the capabilities of certain clouds for specific technologies. For example, an organization may name AWS as its main cloud provider but choose to run big data and analytics on GCP because Google is a pioneer in that space. It may also choose to leverage Azure for its .NET and SQL Server applications or decide that Azure's IoT services are superior. Regardless of the reasons, the software usually does not need to be cloud agnostic. In this model, the platform team supports multiple cloud providers from a single platform.

Regardless of whether the strategy is cloud agnostic or best cloud for the job, the multicloud platform model is becoming increasingly popular. Some enterprises choose to build separate, single-cloud platforms, but many are building cloud platforms that can support multiple cloud providers and are managed with a common set of tools and processes.

HYBRID CLOUD MODEL

The hybrid cloud model is when an enterprise has a mix of both public and private clouds. Although on the surface this looks very much the same as a multi-cloud model, from a technology viewpoint it is very different. Unless the private cloud is managed by a third party, the private cloud implementation requires hardware. Managing physical infrastructure is a different skillset than managing virtual infrastructure in the cloud, even though there is some overlap.

Some enterprises prefer that both on-prem private cloud and public cloud are managed by a single platform team. This requires that the platform team have a wide variety of skills in order to support physical infrastructure and data-center capabilities along with the more software-centric skills of building public cloud platforms. It also requires different operations and support models because of the different responsibilities of the platform team between private and public cloud implementations.

In this model, AWS is responsible for everything from the infrastructure layer down, and the customer is responsible for the middleware layer and the application layer. The cloud platform team takes over that middleware layer and provides a suite of cloud services for their developers. You saw the cloud platform shared responsibility model in Chapter 1 (Figure 1-2).

Figure 6-1 shows the shared responsibility model for the public cloud provider AWS.

Shared responsibility model as an internal cloud provider

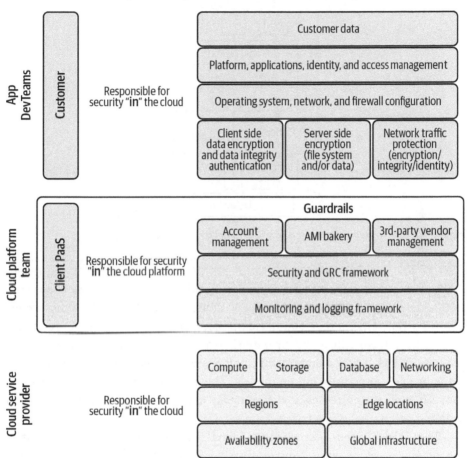

Figure 6-1. Shared responsibility model

The private cloud shared responsibility looks just like the AWS model (Figure 6-1), but without AWS. In other words, the enterprise is responsible for everything. So in a hybrid model, the shared responsibility model looks like Figure 6-2.

Hybrid operating model

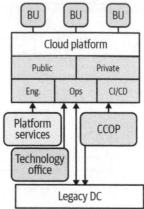

Figure 6-2. Shared responsibility in a hybrid cloud platform model

TWO-SPEED IT

A fourth model is the *two-speed IT* model. In this model, enterprises choose not to mix the traditional way of computing with the ways of the cloud. In this model, if you are not working on cloud-related projects, you interact with the traditional datacenter infrastructure and operations teams. If you are working on cloud-related projects, a new cloud organization is stood up that often drastically redesigns business processes and op models. This is often done to prevent legacy op models, business processes, and technology choices from getting in the way of building optimal solutions in the cloud.

This model is common when the cloud strategy is to build all new apps in the cloud. Therefore, you systematically shrink the on-prem footprint by migrating legacy applications to the cloud over time.

I have also seen this model used for political reasons. For example, it is common to have a VP or C-level person in charge of the datacenter and running the day-to-day business, while a new VP or C-level role is created to drive cloud throughout the organization. The leader of the new cloud role is told to go "break glass" and build new processes and procedures and not be bound by the legacy processes. Although this may create great conflict between the old guard and the new guard, it is often necessary to get the full benefit from the cloud.

Making the Cloud Work for You: Antipatterns and Best Practices

Cloud platforms are key to driving a safe and compliant cloud strategy. When done right, cloud platforms can help organizations realize the promises of cloud computing. They help enterprises manage costs, mitigate risks, drive standards, and accelerate development by abstracting the complexities of cloud infrastructure from developers. When done wrong, cloud platforms can become a crutch for developers that can cause project delays, stifle innovation, lower quality and resilience, and actually negatively impact cloud architectures and services. To avoid these negative consequences, don't go down the paths of these five antipatterns.

CLOUD PLATFORM ANTIPATTERNS

Here are the five antipatterns.

Antipattern 1: If you build it, they will come

This antipattern is common when a company's cloud strategy is being driven by security, governance, or infrastructure teams with little to no input from the development teams. These factions often lack trust in each other, have competing priorities, or even have adversarial relationships.

The result is often a cloud platform that meets the needs of the security, compliance, and operations teams, but not of the developers. *Platforms are for enabling developers.* If the focus of the platform is purely on "preventing developers from doing something stupid," the developer experience will usually suffer. This can lead to poor adoption and even an increase in shadow IT, as developers go elsewhere to get their needs met.

Antipattern 2: Bringing your old tools and processes to the new party

People love their tools. But when standing up a cloud platform, it is critical to select tools that are cloud native, or at least cloud friendly. Before building a cloud platform, you should do an inventory of all of your current tools and the functions that they serve. Then evaluate them against the top tools recommended for the cloud for each function. Some of the existing tools may be a great choice for the cloud; others might not work well, or at all, in a cloud environment. In addition, many older tools come with old processes that no longer make sense in a cloud environment.

Members of one organization used a logging solution from a legacy vendor I had never heard of before. They required the platform team to use it because they didn't want to change their tool. After wasting a lot of time trying to make this tool work properly in the public cloud, they finally gave up—and then required that all logging data be sent to the existing logging solution in the datacenter.

This decision added unnecessary complexity and costs for the platform and did not meet the developers' needs. To make matters worse, the new platform for their public cloud implementation now had a tightly coupled dependency on legacy software and hardware in the datacenter, which was operated by people who were not engaged in the cloud program.

Another organization refused to look at new monitoring solutions and required all cloud traffic to come through the datacenter, first because the web traffic and packet inspection monitoring solutions lived in the datacenter. One day someone attempted to upgrade the software and caused the monitoring solution to go down. This took down all of the company's applications on the public cloud, because no traffic could get to the cloud.

Antipattern 3: Applying worst-case risk profiles to all platform customers

There are a lot of concerns about security and compliance in the cloud—some warranted, some not. In response to security concerns, some organizations implement worst-case scenario policies and controls to the cloud platform.

Not all applications are created equal. If a team is working on an application or service that is handling financial transactions then, heck yeah, be overly conservative and lock everything down as much as possible. But what about the team working on a website that publishes and handles only publicly available information—no financial data or any personally identifiable information (PII)? Why should that team have to go through the same rigorous processes and controls as a payment solution? Too often, platform teams treat all applications, business units, and developers the same even though their requirements may be totally different. Don't treat everything in a binary fashion.

Antipattern 4: Creating new silos and bottlenecks

You create a DevOps team. Now you have a new silo called DevOps, which is just another team the developers have to work with to get work done. Does this sound familiar?

As you learned in Chapter 1, DevOps is not a person, a role, or a team. But too often, companies put a new "DevOps team" in place that manages infrastructure and CI/CD pipelines. That team often has its own set of priorities that don't match those of the development teams.

I was once hired by a product team to help accelerate its cloud project. We had to wait a month for access to their cloud environment, simply because it was not a priority for the DevOps team! In this company, the infrastructure team had simply renamed itself "DevOps" but was not collaborating with the product team, which created unnecessary wait times. One of the main tenets of the DevOps movement is to create a more collaborative environment, so the irony of a new silo called DevOps is not lost on me.

Antipattern 5: Automating waste

Another tenet of DevOps is automation. But before automating "all the things," take the opportunity to reevaluate your current processes.

When software is poorly architected it is usually not reliable which causes a lot of unplanned work. As the quick fixes add up, the architecture continues to degrade. Architects make fun of this with the term *eventual architecture*. Eventual process is similar. You might put a decent process in place to address your current challenges. As the years pass, different issues arise, and quick "fixes" are added to the process to prevent a specific problem from occurring again. Over time, the process becomes so unwieldy that it's almost unrecognizable from its initial inception. People know that the process is inefficient and don't even know why some of the steps are in place, but everyone is afraid to touch it because the whole thing might just collapse.

When you're considering automating a process, it is a good time to perform a value stream mapping exercise to understand the end-to-end flow of the process and where the inefficiencies are. You don't want to automate a process you shouldn't be doing in the first place.

CLOUD PLATFORM BEST PRACTICES

The organizations that have generated business value by implementing a cloud platform embrace many of these best practices.

Best Practice 1: Adopting a product mindset

Platforms should enable developers with self-service capabilities and empower them to deploy and operate their own services. This is a major shift from how we approached ops in the past where developers had to go through the infrastructure and operations teams to get work done. With a product mindset, the operations team focuses on providing reliable services and are not involved in operating the applications on top of the platform.

Instead, the focus is on building a robust service catalog for developers, while embedding safety (security, compliance, cost controls) into the platform. The developers' experience in consuming the platform services should not be cumbersome or time-consuming. Onboarding new developers to the platform should be simple; plenty of training should be available and the platform team should collaborate with the developers to optimize the "customer" experience.

Best Practice 2: Adopting a cloud-provider mindset

Now that you are thinking about the cloud platform as a product, think of the cloud platform team as an internal cloud service provider, much like AWS, Google, or Microsoft. The cloud platform puts the necessary guardrails on top of the cloud provider's solution(s) so that developers can access a secure, compliant, and approved set of cloud services, much like they would if they were logging on to the CSP's own console.

Andy Jassy, CEO of Amazon Web Services (AWS) and a pioneer in cloud computing is known for his obsession with customer experience. I often tell my clients, "WWJD?"—but instead of "What would Jesus do?" I'm asking, "What would Jassy do?"

First, AWS provides a robust service catalog of highly reliable services.

Second, they embed technical experts at their customers' locations to help them learn, architect, and evangelize.

Third, they listen. The cloud providers are really good at deploying new services and features that their customers really need. They are able to do this because they are in the field with customers, walking the halls, talking to architects and business people. They hear firsthand what is working and what is not, what features are missing, or what features have a security gap. All of that information is fed back to the product teams, which influences the product backlog prioritization process so the most relevant features and fixes are quickly launched back to the customers.

The cloud providers invest heavily in training and onboarding their customers. They hold webinars, summits, and conferences. They write whitepapers and blog posts and hold video sessions. Your cloud platform team should do the same. Go to town halls and team meetings to educate and evangelize. Write blog posts, record podcasts, and get included in newsletters and other corporate communication touchpoints.

Most importantly, focus on the customer experience. Remember that your customers are builders, those full-stack teams that are building products and services on top of the cloud platform. One very successful company actually tracks a Net Promoter Score (NPS), which measures how customers view the value of the platform, including the customer experience (which is viewed in terms of developer productivity).

Best Practice 3: Embracing DevOps

Embracing DevOps has been a key factor in all of the successful cloud implementations I have seen over the last several years. The hallmarks of any good DevOps initiative are embracing collaboration across teams with shared goals toward delivering highly resilient systems quickly, safely, and with the customer in mind.

The legacy model of domain silos and processes, built for multiple handoffs between silos, hinders organizations' ability to deliver value in the cloud. As DevOps Research and Assessments (DORA) notes in its 2019 State of DevOps Report (*https://oreil.ly/qddEy*):

> Delivering software quickly, reliably, and safely is at the heart of technology transformation and organizational performance. We see continued evidence that software speed, stability, and availability contribute to organizational performance (including profitability, productivity, and customer satisfaction). Our highest performers are twice as likely to meet or exceed their organizational performance goals.

DORA's 2016 report (*https://oreil.ly/Jelm5*) famously staked the claim that "high-performing IT organizations deploy 30x more frequently with 200x shorter lead times; they have 60x fewer failures and recover 168x faster."

All of the research and customer case studies lead to one obvious conclusion: that DevOps plays a critical role in delivering better software faster, and in increasing the odds of success for any cloud initiative.

Best Practice 4: Embracing a minimal viable cloud (MVC) approach

Building a cloud platform can be a daunting task. One mistake I have seen organizations make is to spend a year or two trying to build the perfect cloud platform, complete with every single policy and control that exists in the current datacenter. The business has to put its cloud journey on hold while everyone waits for the platform to become available; worse, sometimes they start building their own capabilities because they just can't wait.

Instead of "going dark" on the business, pick one or two applications as your first candidates to use the cloud platform. Build only the minimal set of guardrails required to get those applications into the cloud. In heavily regulated industries, it is common to start with applications that don't have personally identifiable data or financial data, to minimize the scope of the controls for version 1.0 of the platform. This allows the organization to get the platform ready in months instead of years. Once the apps are deployed on the platform, pick a few more apps and add the necessary guardrails for those. Continue iterating through this process to bring more workloads to the cloud.

This reiterates the need to approach the cloud platform with a product mindset. Have a roadmap and continuously add features and services to add value for the customers. This is exactly how the cloud providers approach it: one service or feature at a time.

Best Practice 5: Designing different engagement models for different customer categories

This is the flip side of antipattern 3, "Apply worst-case risk profiles to all platform customers." Not only do applications have different risk profiles, but customers have different levels of technical capability.

Too often I see platform teams design with the least knowledgeable customer in mind, creating a lot of processes to protect them from doing the wrong things. The problem is that this slows down the cloud-savvy group with processes that are, for them, unnecessary. Cloud platform teams should meet their customers where they are.

In the next section, we'll look at the types of cloud customers and the engagement models that work best for each type.

Choosing the Right Model for Your Cloud Maturity Level

We just covered a lot of ground. In the last two chapters, you've learned about the three types of operating models (centralized, decentralized, and federated), the factors that drive decisions about them, and their antipatterns and best practices. You've also learned about cloud platform models, engagement models, cloud governance, cloud platform patterns, and platform support models. This can seem overwhelming. There are so many possible permutations! The most important thing is to pick a combination of models and start. The models you pick on day one will look drastically different than your model in year two.

It is critical that you start with a model you can implement within the constraints of your company culture. You can tweak it over time as you, and your organization, learn more and gain cloud maturity. This is common among enterprises starting their cloud journey.

Here's an example from my experience. A large healthcare company I'll call CareCo started with a private cloud implementation a few years before it decided to embrace the public cloud. A new leader was assigned to lead the public cloud initiative, but was forced to work within the constraints of the existing private cloud operating model, which was very infrastructure focused. The new leader wanted to leverage cloud native services, including third-party PaaS solutions and fully managed analytics services from Google. It took much politicking, but eventually they obtained permission to move CareCo away from the hybrid cloud model and build a new single-cloud platform specifically for Google Cloud Platform.

Similarly, a large financial institution I'll call Chatham Finance started its cloud journey with AWS and built its platform with the single purpose of adopting AWS's cloud-native services. Three years later, as Chatham Finance became more mature in its cloud capabilities, it started exploring GCP for analytics workloads and Azure for IoT. Eventually, Chatham extended its cloud platform to support all three cloud providers, moving to a multicloud model.

Both companies found that their priorities and needs changed as they learned more about their options and gained cloud maturity. Yours will, too. The key takeaway is: pick a cloud platform model and expect it to change over time as your cloud journey evolves. Too many companies don't get started because they spend countless months in "analysis paralysis," unwilling to start until they can create the perfect model. There is no perfect model. Start somewhere and continually improve.

Conclusion

This concludes your tour of the cloud platform, in the variety of forms that it can take. As you move through your cloud adoption journey, you'll be making crucial decisions about how to structure your platform; it's my hope that these chapters will help you find the right fit and avoid common errors. Remember, none of these decisions, as important as they are, are written in stone. Life in the cloud is all about change, so be prepared to change your models and strategies as you gain cloud maturity and come to better understand what you and your consumers need.

Once you've got a plan, it's time for implementation. Are you ready to get off the ground? The next chapter will give you an overview of cloud operations, with a particular emphasis on site reliability engineering.

7

Cloud Operations and Reliability

This chapter will focus on operations in the cloud. I've mentioned more than once—because it's important—that a cloud platform team should think and act like a cloud service provider: focused on the product and with an unwavering commitment to customer satisfaction. It also means making security and compliance core competencies of the platform. This new mindset requires a different approach: one that views operations through the eyes of a cloud service provider.

As of September 2020, AWS had almost two hundred services to choose from. Customers can use as many or as few of them as they wish. Some customers only use basic IaaS services like compute, network, and storage; others go all the way up the stack and use fully managed services for technologies like blockchain, IoT, analytics, and gaming. AWS does not know or care how customers build on top of its platform. Its goal is to make sure the platform it provides meets its service levels, so customers can build on it and meet *their* service levels.

One main goal of the platform team is to drive adoption measured in usage of the platform, both at the overall platform level and the service level. Cloud providers accomplish this through many means, including evangelism, training, embedding architects to help with solutioning, and others. But probably the most important thing they do to drive adoption is providing easy-to-use and reliable services that customers can count on. This, in essence, is the goal of platform operations. A good mission statement for a platform team would be:

> *Create a safe, reliable, and easy-to-use platform that enables builders to create business value at speed.*

The key word in this mission statement is *enable*. Too often platforms are built to *control* developers. I touched on this in Chapter 5, when we discussed preventative and empowering approaches to platform culture. I have seen too many platform teams try to create templates, blueprints, and patterns for every use case imaginable to prevent development teams from creating bad architectures or making poor design decisions. This usually results in one of two outcomes. The first is analysis paralysis, where the team wastes countless cycles trying to solve for every use case. The second, which is even worse, is that they create an overprescriptive platform that becomes too cumbersome for the developers. So, as we asked in Chapter 6, what would Jassy do? Jassy would focus on creating the best damn services on the planet *and* creating a robust customer community-relations team that teaches, evangelizes, advises, and architects for its customers. While engaging with customers, the platform teams create a feedback loop with the product team that can use what they learn from that engagement to continuously improve the platform services and prioritize the backlog to deliver what customers need most. Your cloud platform approach should mimic this.

In this chapter, I'll focus on how to run what you build in the cloud. How do you operate the cloud platform? How do your developers operate their applications and services? And how can you ensure reliability of the platform and its services?

Modern Approaches to Platform Operations

As more workloads move onto the cloud platform, platform teams must maintain their service-level agreements (SLAs) with their customers. For example, if Azure announces the release of a new machine learning API, the platform team needs to ensure that adding this new service, and handling the additional cloud consumption it attracts, has no impact on any other services.

Part of what this means is that the platform team must bring the team's capacity up to match the forecasted demand. However, meeting demand does not necessarily mean hiring more people at scale. That might happen, but this need should also drive higher levels of automation, including those that use artificial intelligence (AI), which I will discuss later in the chapter, in the section "Monitoring and AIOps."

Platform operations is the end-to-end management of a cloud platform with a product-centric mindset. It involves three major roles: operating the technology stack (TechOps), managing the catalog of cloud services offered on the platform (service catalog management), and fulfilling service requests (request management). Keep in mind that these are *roles*, not necessarily teams or people.

Tip

It's easy to confuse operations with operating models. *Operations* describes what you actually *do*, while *operating models* describes the plan for how to do it. So *platform operations* is the end-to-end management of a cloud platform with a product-centric mindset; the *platform operating model* is the structure of that cloud platform.

TECHOPS

TechOps is the part of operations that involves monitoring the cloud platform to ensure performance, reliability, and agreed-upon service levels with customers, both internal and external. TechOps includes managing the IaaS and PaaS layers of the cloud platform, monitoring the security framework, and financial monitoring (often called FinOps).

The TechOps role does not focus on building platform services. That role belongs to cloud engineering. Cloud engineering builds the platform; TechOps runs it.

Again, these are roles, not groups. In smaller teams or organizations just starting their cloud journey, there is often a single team that performs both functions. When cloud programs reach a certain scale, they generally dedicate people or teams to these specific roles, either separately or as a single team with these distinct roles embedded.

TechOps is the term I like to use, but some enterprises call this CloudOps, DevOps, or many other names. It can get confusing, and I recommend clearly defining the terms you use to reduce confusion. Call this function what you want, as long as your goal is to provide reliable services to your customers and timely turnaround time for their requests.

SERVICE CATALOG MANAGEMENT

A service catalog is the list of cloud services available to cloud consumers within the cloud platform. The person or people responsible for it manage the catalog and the institutional knowledge it represents. They define what services are available, maintain those services, and provide documentation and training for those who use the catalog and its services. They also communicate changes, updates, and plans to stakeholders across the enterprise.

Service catalog management is often a core responsibility of an established CCOP.

REQUEST MANAGEMENT

The platform team receives numerous requests every day. Here's an example of what the incoming requests might look like on a typical day:

- Requests for access to the platform or to a specific account, group, or service

- Requests for infrastructure: this might include firewall changes, patches, and new environments like sandboxes or test environments.

- Requests for training or knowledge transfer

- Requests for troubleshooting and other help

- Requests to onboard new users or services onto the platform

- Requests to respond to incidents and outages on the platform

Some organizations fold this role into TechOps, but I prefer separating the two into dedicated teams (budgets aside), because they are different skillsets.

People in the TechOps role are typically, or should be, highly skilled cloud engineers. When they get bogged down in daily requests and don't get to perform the technical tasks they enjoy and are certified for, they often experience lower morale and even burnout from working long hours to satisfy the demand for both operations and request management. Many such engineers leave to seek opportunities where they can focus on using their skills.

Another reason for the separation is that the requests are mostly unplanned work. If the engineers are splitting time between their normal operations and unplanned work from incoming requests, it can become challenging for them to find sufficient time to perform their operations duties. Even worse, the priority conflicts and context switching involved in juggling the two can result in the time to service a request becoming too slow. This may, in turn, lead to subpar operations performance, drastically impacting the cloud adoption process overall.

I have seen service requests for simple tasks, such as provisioning an environment, take *months*. Why? First, as I mentioned in the previous chapters, bringing your old tools and processes to the cloud can be a major bottleneck. Second, the fulfillment process of that request may not yet be automated. (More about automation later in this chapter.) Third, the same people responsible for service catalog management and TechOps are also responsible for fulfilling requests: another huge bottleneck.

As you build out these functions within your cloud platform, make sure you have the proper automation in place and the right amount of resources and bandwidth to meet customers' expectations. No one should have to wait months for something they could easily have done themselves in ten minutes.

Site Reliability Engineering

Managing cloud platform operations requires balancing daily operations tasks with building tooling, operations features, and automation to accommodate scaling requirements. Remember, the cloud platform is a product. Products that are unreliable will fail due to low customer satisfaction and trust. One could argue that reliability is the most important feature of a cloud platform: without it, you have no customers, and thus you have no product.

So how can platform teams balance the twin priorities of operating a reliable platform and building new features for customers? Google perfected the balancing act with an approach they call *site reliability engineering* (SRE).

Whether systems are migrated to the cloud or built there greenfield style, their reliability can make or break cloud adoption for a company. I have witnessed companies with strong brands and websites with a long history of high reliability and availability moving to the cloud only to suffer numerous outages and become very unreliable. Each time I have seen this occur, the company's executives start questioning the viability of the cloud migration as a whole. In a few instances, they decided to migrate back to on-prem and abandon the public cloud altogether. But it was never the cloud that was at fault for the outages and reliability issues. It was a combination of bad architecture and an unprepared operations team.

So how can operations teams change their mindset for the cloud?

Traditionally, the teams that build a product and the teams that operate that product have conflicting goals and incentives. Operations teams' goals and objectives are typically aligned to reliability, security, and compliance, which are measured across the multiple product teams they support. Product teams, by contrast, are typically measured on speed to market, number of features and enhancements delivered, and customer satisfaction. Operations favors stability and minimal change, while product favors constant change. These two sets of goals are in direct conflict. What gives?

Google delivers products and services at large scale. It found that traditional methods of operating large, complex systems produced subpar results. To balance the goals of reliability and speed to market at scale, it created the concept of

SRE. Benjamin Treynor Sloss, the senior VP overseeing technical operations at Google, coined the term. He famously defined SRE (*https://oreil.ly/hAtYw*) as "what happens when you ask a software engineer to design an operations function." Google's philosophy is that operations work should be highly automated. It purposely hires engineers because, Sloss says, they "are inherently both predisposed to, and have the ability to, substitute automation for human labor." Google SREs can all write code.

The SRE team is usually a mix of software engineers and people who have infrastructure and operations backgrounds but can also code. Their goals are simple: apply automation wherever possible and feasible, eliminate toil, maximize change velocity as much as possible without violating service-level objectives (SLOs), and continuously drive reliability for the systems and services they support. Google also measures what SREs work on, because they have a core principle that SREs spend half their time operating the systems and the other half improving the reliability of the system.

Simply copying Google's SRE model is not recommended; most organizations do not have the same talent and scalability challenges as Google does. Instead, understand what problems Google is solving with SRE and what their guiding principles are. Then design your own model and implementation of SRE to fit *your* culture, talent, and systems. SRE is a great concept for helping product teams deliver and maintain highly reliable systems and services. Focus on the goals of reliability and speed to market, not how Google does it. Learn from them and adapt what can work in your organization.

Let's discuss some key terms. I mentioned reducing toil already. *Toil* is "the kind of work tied to running a production service that tends to be manual, repetitive, automatable, tactical, devoid of enduring value, and that scales linearly as a service grows."[1] Toil is found not just in technical parts of the system but often in processes. Toil can include meetings, filling out forms, approvals, and other processes that could be easily eliminated with automation and built into a trusted system, such as a CI/CD pipeline with security and code scans.

Let's look at some of the most important concepts in SRE:

---

1 Niall Richard Murphy, Betsy Beyer, Chris Jones, and Jennifer Petoff, *Site Reliability Engineering: How Google Runs Production Systems* (O'Reilly), Chapter 5.

Service-level agreements (SLAs)

A service-level agreement is a promise a supplier makes to customers: it's a contractual obligation for the expected level of service that a product will provide. The SLA may come with guarantees and penalties if the service levels are not met. For example, AWS publishes the SLA for its compute instances known as EC2 (Elastic Compute Cloud): 99.99% monthly uptime, which equates to 4.38 minutes of downtime a year. If AWS does not meet that SLA, it must provide service credits to the customer.

Service-level indicators (SLIs)

A service-level indicator is the data that shows how you are performing against your SLOs: it's a quantitative measure of some aspect of a service level, such as latency, error rate, throughput, availability, or durability.

Service-level objectives (SLOs)

Service-level objectives are the objectives a team must meet to support the SLA. An SLO is usually a target value (or range of values) measured by an SLI. For example, an SLO might be that average latency must be less than or equal to 100 milliseconds, that availability must be at least 99.9% in any given 24-hour period, or that at least 90% of requests must complete within 400 milliseconds.

SLOs measure the overall health of a service. They are used for internal purposes and are not shared with customers.

Error budget agreements

An error budget is a method to help prioritize engineering work in balance with innovation work (reliability versus new features, as you'll recall) by spelling out exactly how much unreliability is acceptable. For example, if your SLO says that a service must have 99.9% availability (often called "three nines" of availability), it means you are allowing for roughly 40 minutes of downtime a month. If an incident occurs that makes the service unavailable for 10 minutes, you've just burned 25% of your error budget for the month. When availability degrades to below three nines, or more than 40 minutes, your agreed-upon *error budget* with the product owner dictates that improving reliability should now be prioritized above creating new features.

Too often, engineering user stories that improve the overall reliability of a system yield priority to features, with the engineering tasks pushed back to another day—resulting in more technical debt. Even well-architected systems can run into issues when they encounter loads like they've never experienced before. Events like these can create unplanned work and drive the need for a lot of quick fixes to maintain service levels.

Without an approach like SRE, these quick fixes live on forever while more quick and dirty fixes are added to the product. Eventually the technical debt piles up to the point where the system becomes too hard to maintain, and getting new features out the door becomes challenging due to the increase in unplanned work. I call this the "never-ending cycle of doom": there is never time to do things right but always enough time to do things wrong. In the cycle of doom, not only is firefighting the norm, it's actually rewarded.

Instead of rewarding firefighting, we should reward fire prevention. SRE error budgets are the fire prevention techniques that allow enterprises to move away from constant firefighting. They give both the product owner and the engineers a way to maintain reliability while delivering features fast.

I recommend implementing reliability engineering for the cloud platform and leveraging error budgets. The TechOps role should be split between operating the platform and improving overall reliability. Google targets a 50-50 split between operations and reliability engineering, but again, don't merely copy that number. Your initial target should be based on how reliable your current platform is, how much manual intervention is required, and your current staffing level versus the immediate demand. You may need to start by spending a higher percentage of your time on operations. However, if you skip error budgeting, your odds of ever getting to a 50-50 split are very low. You will most likely be battling toil endlessly.

In the sections that follow, I'll focus on helping you understand the operating models for SRE, as well as some of the antipatterns that arise when implementing it.

Tip

Site reliability engineering is a huge topic, and many books are devoted to it. While a deep dive is outside the scope of this book, I encourage you to learn more about SRE. Here are some good places to start:

- Heather Adkins, Betsy Beyer, Paul Blankinship, Piotr Lewandowski, Ana Oprea, and Adam Stubblefield, *Building Secure and Reliable Systems: Best Practices for Designing, Implementing, and Maintaining Systems* (O'Reilly)

- Niall Richard Murphy, Betsy Beyer, Chris Jones, and Jennifer Petoff, *Site Reliability Engineering: How Google Runs Production Systems* (O'Reilly)

- Michael Nygard, *Release It!: Design and Deploy Production-Ready Software* (Pragmatic Bookshelf)

THE MANY MISSIONS OF SITE RELIABILITY ENGINEERS

SRE has been implemented in many different forms with varying missions and structures (known as SRE operating models). Here are some of the missions I have seen most often over the last few years:

Full-service SREs
> Google refers to this as "kitchen sink." In this kind of team, the scope of SRE is unbounded. These engineers work on ops, infrastructure, tooling, and whatever else it takes to support the reliability of a product or service. This is common in enterprises where the product team owns both development and operations, whereas the SRE team is funded by and dedicated to the product.

Application SREs
> These reliability engineers focus on the application software, not the underlying infrastructure. They live above the hypervisor and have expert knowledge of the product or products they support. This is common when a company has an established cloud platform team that provides infrastructure services to the product teams. Infrastructure is often a key component

of application reliability, so the application SREs work closely with the platform team to align on the product's infrastructure needs.

Platform SREs

Also called infrastructure SREs, these SREs are responsible for the reliability of the cloud services provided by the cloud platform. For hybrid cloud or private cloud implementations, they also focus heavily on physical infrastructure, not just cloud services.

Incident management REs

Companies like Netflix leave service reliability to the individual product teams, but implement an overarching reliability team that manages incidents across all services that make up the product (in Netflix's case, streaming videos). These SREs don't own and operate infrastructure, support individual services, or participate in deployments. Instead, when something goes wrong, they take charge. They manage the incident, then perform analysis afterward to learn from the incident and improve the overall reliability of the product.

SRE OPERATING MODELS

In addition to the types of SREs, there are different organizational structures for leveraging SRE resources. Let's look at a few of the most important:

One-to-one

In the one-to-one model, an SRE team is assigned to a single product. This is a common model for products that require high scalability or for mission-critical applications whose reliability is crucial to the business.

This model falls into the "you build it, you run it" category, where dedicated dev and SRE team goals are aligned to the overall goals of the product. The advantage of this model is the SRE team acquires deep knowledge of the product from focusing exclusively on it. The downside of this model is it doesn't scale. You will never be able to hire enough talent to field a dedicated SRE team for each product.

One-to-many (1toM)

In this model, the SRE team supports multiple products and services. For example, an SRE team might be assigned to a business unit and support all applications in that BU's portfolio that require dedicated reliability engineering.

The advantage of this model is economies of scale. Precious SRE resources can provide more coverage across more products. The downside is that the SRE team cannot provide the singular focus on a product that the one-to-one model provides. BUs often fund a dedicated SRE team or teams for their portfolio of applications. It is also not uncommon for a BU to have a dedicated SRE team for a mission-critical app, and a one-to-many arrangement for the rest of the portfolio.

Embedded

In this model there is no SRE team that exists independently. Instead, one or more reliability engineers are *part* of the development team. They become deeply knowledgeable about the product they support and engage with the architects to build in reliability and operability early in the life cycle.

The advantage of this model is that there are no silos. The SRE is part of the development team with a specific focus on reliability, which makes goals and priority alignment easy. The downside is the difficulty of scaling this model: only certain products will be fortunate enough to have their own dedicated SREs.

SRE as a service

This is the classical shared service model, where SREs operate as a Community of Practice, training and sharing best practices. (This goes by many names; "Center of Excellence" is also common.) Product teams request SRE resources from this central body when they need them.

This model offers more standardization of best practices, and the SREs get exposed to a broader set of applications. The downside is that it assumes the SRE will acquire deep knowledge of the product during their stint working on it, which is not always true. Also, shared service models create dependencies on other teams and can force teams to contend for resources.

IMPLEMENTING SRE IN THE ENTERPRISE

Implementing SRE can work as a bottom-up, grassroots effort or as a top-down, C-level-driven effort. Some of the most successful implementations of SRE I have seen have come from the grassroots, where a team adopted SRE to address scalability issues in one of its systems.

Bottom-up SRE implementations

When SRE adoption is driven by a need or a significant event, this creates a sense of urgency and tends to increase the odds of a successful adoption. Adopting SRE because it is in fashion is much harder, because the "why" is harder to define. That does not mean you need to wait for a compelling event to adopt SRE; you just need to map your SRE implementation to some measure of business value. Remember, positive events can strain the system as much as negative events can. For example, you might anticipate an unprecedented strain on your systems if you expect a substantial year-over-year increase in customer onboarding for your SaaS product, or a fivefold increase in web traffic during the holiday season. To prepare for those crucial events, you might well want to embrace a leading approach for providing high reliability, which would be a very good reason to adopt SRE.

Top-down SRE implementations

Driving SRE adoption from the top down can be challenging, especially if there are no prior SRE success stories or pilots underway. Too often, companies create an SRE center of excellence (COE) or similar body and start defining standards and tooling from the start, before the reliability engineers can gain any practical hands-on experience working with developers and product owners. Some COEs spend months creating strategies based on a set of hypotheses about how SRE should work within their company, without any feedback from developers or product owners. After all those months of strategy, they still aren't offering anything that meets the BUs' and dev teams' needs, so they find it extremely hard to get buy-in.

A better approach is to pick a product that needs reliability engineering and has a very strong team that is willing to embrace change. Start small and run some experiments with this team by implementing the basic concepts of SRE. Create a safe environment where teams can try new things and openly share feedback on what worked and what failed, in a blameless setting. Once the team starts maturing with SRE, you can start establishing best practices. Instead of setting up a command-and-control style COE, consider a cloud community of practice (CCOP) model (discussed in Chapter 5), where the leaders work with the community to continuously refine SRE best practices so that future teams can learn from them.

The central team approach, whether it is the traditional COE model or the CCOP model I prefer, should not be a rigid governance body. Instead, the central team should be evangelists, educators, coaches, and subject matter experts. They should produce guiding principles, recommend standards and best practices, and manage and measure SRE adoption across the enterprise. Their goal should *not* be to control and govern SRE adoption. A better approach is to set a vision and drive SRE adoption through coaching, mentoring, assisting, and continuously refining the guidelines based on feedback from the community. You might also consider taking the reliability engineers from the early pilot teams, who are now the company's experts, and either embedding them into new teams or having them act as advisors or coaches to the teams. I've seen both approaches accelerate successful SRE adoptions.

Candidate Systems for SRE

Enterprises usually implement SRE for high-scale web applications, like ecommerce sites; important sites like the company's brand page that support large amounts of web traffic; and SaaS solutions that support many enterprise customers. But even though "site" is in the name of site reliability engineering, you don't need a web-facing product or service to adopt the principles of SRE.

In fact, unless you are only using SRE for websites, I recommend dropping "site" and just calling it reliability engineering. Many companies substitute the first initial of their company. For example, our fictitious company MediaCo from Chapter 4 might call it MRE, for MediaCo Reliability Engineering. Names may seem trivial, but in large enterprises, messaging is extremely important in getting people to adopt new ways of working and of prioritizing work (like error budgets). "SRE" sounds like another IT buzzword, but if you tell them you want to improve reliability and reduce technical debt, you are more likely to get cooperation.

Successful SRE implementations usually start with products that are already fairly reliable. Products that have major stability and reliability issues are not great places to start SRE. SRE can't fix bad architecture, poorly implemented Agile practices, immature IT processes, and other problems. If you are working on unreliable systems, fix those issues first before trying to tackle advanced ways of operating products at scale, like SRE.

Good candidate systems for SRE include systems that require high levels of reliability, those that support infrastructure and platforms that provide services to product teams, and greenfield cloud native applications. Let's take a closer look at why SRE works well for these systems:

Systems with high reliability requirements

Some systems are mission-critical: their reliability has a major impact on revenue and customer retention. These might include online banking applications, a company's .com website, an ecommerce site, a social media application, or a hotel reservation system. Because the balance between new features and engineering tasks that improve reliability can make or break a product, these types of systems can greatly benefit from embracing SRE.

Infrastructure and platforms

Teams that provide infrastructure as a service and cloud platform teams that serve multiple teams and business units must provide highly reliable service levels, because the product teams (those building on top of the infrastructure or platforms) depend on these services. The product is only as reliable as the infrastructure or platform underlying it, so if the product teams can't trust the underlying infrastructure or platforms, they will take matters into their own hands and start creating their own "shadow IT" teams. This, as you learned in Chapter 1, can create all kinds of risks around security, governance, and financial management.

Greenfield cloud native applications

What better way to implement SRE than to do it with a new team working on a new product, without any legacy constraints from existing systems? Cloud native products can be a good place to start cultivating an SRE team within your organization.

SRE ANTIPATTERNS

Before I move into the details of how SRE teams plan for the unexpected, I want to share with you some antipatterns to avoid.

Antipattern 1: Renaming operations to "SRE"

This is the most common antipattern I see in my work. Operations team members read all the books, watch all the talks, and then change their titles and team name to SRE—without changing much else.

They still operate in a silo, they go wild automating "all the things" without fixing process issues first, and they still focus on tools above all. They are still not operating as part of a product team or as a partner to the developers. It's the same old ops team with a new name. Sometimes they even rename their ops team "DevOps," only to change it to "SRE" a year or two later.

Antipattern 2: Having the infrastructure team create an SRE shared service

Central IT teams often get used to being the approval gate for anything that goes to production, whether it is code or infrastructure. Some of these teams like to start SRE initiatives with the desire to own reliability and maintain control of release management, without any alignment to the goals and objectives of the product teams they serve. They look to automate things to eliminate toil in their world, infrastructure, and often own and mandate the CI/CD tooling and standards. In organizations where central IT has absolute authority over product teams, they strongly enforce their tools and processes, providing a list of "services" for the product teams to use. In organizations where they don't have total control, they fall into the "build it and they will come" debacle (as you saw in Chapter 6), where they build what's good for them but nobody adopts it because it does not meet their needs. (But hey, it sure looks good on a LinkedIn profile!)

Antipattern 3: Conflating automation with SRE

Often teams conflate automation initiatives with SRE. They form a team that focuses on automating everything they can, but don't bother with SLOs, SLIs, and error budgets. Automating things can create better reliability, but automation by itself is not enough. There is nothing wrong with an initiative to increase automation, just don't mistake it for SRE.

Antipattern 4: Loading the SRE team with developers who have no operations or infrastructure experience

The makeup of an SRE team should include a combination of operations skills and development skills. While Google might have engineers with extensive experience in both areas, that is not the norm. Make sure the SRE team has a good mix of skill sets, because reliable systems are typically built with operations in mind. If nobody on the team has a background in ops or infrastructure, the odds of prioritizing engineering to increase reliability are low, and the odds of effectively managing or preventing incidents are even lower.

RELIABILITY VERSUS RESILIENCE: BEST PRACTICES

People often confuse the terms *reliability* and *resilience*. I define *reliability* as a system's ability to function as it was intended, when it is expected, and wherever the customer is. I define *resilience* as how well a system, including the people within it, responds to adversity. Reliability focuses on keeping systems running smoothly, while resilience focuses on reacting to incidents and events while minimizing their impact on the customer experience.

You can define reliability with SLOs, measure it with SLIs, and monitor these measures proactively to head off issues before they become visible to the user. But once an issue occurs that impacts your metrics, the ability to recover or respond quickly can make or break your SLOs.

Reliability engineering is half of the equation. The other half is addressing resilience. You have to architect for resilience. Resilience is not an incident management process. To build resilient systems you must anticipate and design for failures. Resilience requires deep knowledge of the application or service that you are trying to make resilient. Resilience can be improved with design decisions at every layer of the architecture, which is why full-stack teams that focus on a product are better suited to create highly resilient systems, especially when they also have shared incentives and a product owner who adheres to error budgets.

When *everybody* owns and is measured on reliability and resilience—not just the infrastructure, SRE, or developer teams—then you can start looking at your system more holistically instead of making patchwork fixes. Since developers and SREs work closely together, they have a unique opportunity to collaborate in building in high levels of resilience throughout the entire stack. This is true for each of the SRE types I mentioned earlier. Application SREs are immersed in the application and can help bring a "design for operations" approach to the table earlier in the life cycle. Platform SREs can work closely with product teams to provide best platform services, developer tools, and more visibility into system health and performance. Incident management SREs research the incidents and provide knowledge and recommendations for prevention and recovery of incidents to improve resilience.

There are many ways to improve the overall resilience of a system by dealing better with adversity—known broadly as *stability patterns*. I'll discuss a few here briefly, but the architectural details are outside the scope of this book.[2] Now for that quick overview.

Best Practice 1: Build in retries

Most cloud systems are complex, made up of numerous infrastructure components communicating over the internet, which is made up of still other communication mechanisms. Each interaction between the software and the hardware over a communication channel is a potential point of failure. Connections drop,

---

2 If you want to learn more, I highly recommend reading Michael Nygard, *Release It!* (Pragmatic Bookshelf).

messages fail, servers hang, and anything that can happen will happen. *Building in the ability to retry* can prevent a system from failing.

There is nothing new here. We have been doing this since the mainframe days. What is new is that applications are more complex and the software is running outside of our datacenters, over communications channels we don't own and control. The result is that there are many more potential points of failure: this makes capturing errors and performing retries more critical than ever.

Best Practice 2: Checkpoint long-running transactions or units of work

If, like me, you were developing on mainframes back in the '80s, you will be very familiar with checkpoint/restart. For everyone else, let me explain. If any transaction or job is expected to take a long time, it is a best practice to *capture the successful work completed along the way* so that if the job fails, you can start where you left off.

Picture a customer applying for a loan online. This flow is pictured in Figure 7-1.

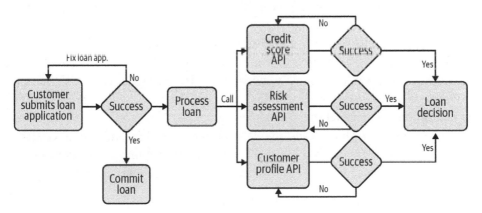

Figure 7-1. Checkpoints within an API flow

The loan process might include five or six steps that require the customer to provide data (such as their annual income and Social Security number). After the customer enters the data, the system commits it to some storage medium (such as a database or a cookie) and calls three APIs to determine if the loan is approved and at what rate: a credit score service, a risk-assessment service, and a customer profile service. These three APIs return data to a final service that determines the approval and the acceptable rate.

If any API fails, an acceptable number of retries will be made (without the customer's knowledge). When the APIs return data successfully, it is stored and sent to the loan approval API service. If the loan approval API fails at this step, it is also retried. The loan approval API will reject the loan if the results it receives from the credit score, risk score, or customer profile API don't meet the minimum requirements; for example, if the credit score API returns a score of 525, there is no need to evaluate the other values. The customer must pass the criteria for all three requirements.

The architect has two decisions here. The architect can choose to call the three qualifying APIs sequentially or process them all in parallel. The advantage of processing them sequentially is that if the customer fails to achieve the requirements of the first call, there is no need to call the other two APIs. This approach can reduce the overall number of calls the system makes each day, which can have a major positive impact to system performance if the system is processing millions of loans a day. However, if loan applications have a high success rate, let's say 95%, then you are not saving many calls, and math might work out to show that it is better to process the three APIs in parallel to improve the response time back to the customer.

For example, let's say that the third-party credit score API is known to have performance issues and can sometimes take up to a second to respond. The other two APIs average a 250-ms response time. If we use the sequential process, it could take 1.5 seconds to retrieve the data plus the time the loan process takes to determine the approval status and loan rate.

You have to weigh the trade-offs between response time and system capacity and costs. Regardless, performing checkpoints to commit finished work in a long transaction can save time and improve the overall customer experience.

Best Practice 3: Keep things independent

I discussed this topic in my first book, *Architecting the Cloud* (Wiley). The concept here is to architect a system so that key components of the system are isolated from the effects of reliability issues in other components. This should be designed with the customer experience in mind.

I worked at a startup back in 2008 that offered and redeemed digital customer incentives like coupons, rebates, and ads. The system had three major components: the customer-facing website that we built for each retailer, a B2B system for exchanging digital content with the content providers, and a redemption engine that processed offers at the point of sale in real time. Each of these three major components was deployed on its own infrastructure and scaled independently. In addition, each retailer was deployed on its own infrastructure with its own database, so that no retailer would be affected by any issue or by a traffic spike resulting from a problem elsewhere in the system. This increased our costs and management complexity, but our top priorities were performance, high reliability, and resilience.

Best Practice 4: Focus on perceived performance

Designing for perceived performance is more of an art than a science. You need deep knowledge not only of the application but of the customer experience. *Perceived performance* is a measure of performance *as experienced by the customer*, not the actual performance of the system. Going back to my point of sale example: when a customer is at the register at a store, items are scanned one at a time. Every time an item is scanned, systems are computing discounts, prices, inventory, and various other processes. When the cashier hits the total button, the order is tallied, the discounts and taxes are applied, and the receipt is printed. The perceived performance of that system is the time it takes from when the cashier hits total to when the consumer gets their receipt. Under the hood, there is a lot of processing going on, including, in this case, a call to our systems running on AWS to determine what digital offers are available to be redeemed.

The customer expects to see the receipt in a few seconds. We had an SLA to return in a few hundred milliseconds. Working with perceived performance gave us opportunities to apply a lot of tricks to accommodate failures and still meet the customers' expectations. We allowed for retries, cached data in preparation of a customer shopping, and finally designed an offline exception process that would let the transaction continue if our system was unable to respond. The offline process would not make that customer happy, but nothing makes a retailer more angry than slowing down their cashiers—so instead of continually trying to correct the issue, we offloaded the customer to a service desk or mobile application for resolution.

Here is a simpler example. Let's say ACME Shipping has a package-tracking service. When a customer asks to see the status of their package, the tracking service calls three APIs. One gets the customer information, the second gets the package location, and the third gets the package history.

Here's how that history works. The package's last known history is stored in the package history database. When the user enters the tracking number, the tracking service calls the package location service. If it does not return after three retries, the tracking service looks up the customer from the customer service API using the tracking number, then gets the last known package location from the package history service. The tracking service returns the last known location with an "as of" date.

The system may be encountering an outage for the package location service, but it can hide that because a last known status is acceptable from the customer's perspective. They perceive that the tracking service responded in an acceptable amount of time. So although the underlying components of the system may not have met their SLOs, the system's method of accommodating an expected failure helped keep it resilient.

There are two key takeaways here. First, *focusing on reliability is not good enough—you need resilience, too.* No matter how reliable a system is, if it does not respond well to adversity, the customer's perception of the overall system will suffer. Second, to improve resilience effectively, the collective team must have in-depth knowledge not only of the software and hardware components, but also the customers' experience and expectations.

For systems with high scalability and performance requirements, though, we still need to do more to ensure reliability and resilience. We've talked about designs for expected issues and outages, but how do we handle the unknowns? We need to rethink the way we test and the way we operate.

Planning for the Unexpected

As I have hammered home throughout this book, you can't bring your old tools and processes to the cloud and expect great results. Building software in the cloud is an exercise in distributed computing, where the infrastructure scales horizontally on demand. Monitoring distributed, immutable, and elastic cloud-based infrastructure is very different from monitoring a mainframe system or a three-tier architecture with a web, application, and database server that can only scale horizontally and must always be up.

But the complexity does not end at the infrastructure layer. Container-based architectures, serverless architectures, microservices, hybrid cloud architectures, and numerous other approaches present new challenges. When we built code with monolithic architectures, we could walk through our code with a debugger and easily trace the flow of traffic as messages traverse our three-tier architecture. But how do you monitor a complex system that may spawn a collection of containers with microservices that call AWS Lambda functions that query a table on an AWS fully managed database? A single unit of work in this type of architecture may make 20 or 30 hops across the network, leveraging multiple microservices written by different teams and deployed at different times. There is no single code base to troubleshoot. There is no known pattern of traffic to monitor.

Figure 7-2 shows a heuristic developed in the aerospace industry that has since filtered out into risk management of all kinds: the Knowns and Unknowns framework (*https://oreil.ly/mZePF*). It divides risks into four categories, based on what people are aware of and what they understand.

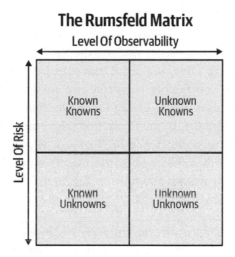

Figure 7-2. *The Knowns and Unknowns framework in the cloud*

Known knowns

The "known knowns" are things you are aware of and understand: everyone knows that car accidents are a common risk, so we plan for them with airbags and seatbelts and antilock brakes. In computing, a good example might be a server failure. Traditional, metric-based monitoring tools are great for dealing with the known knowns.

Known unknowns

The "known unknowns" are risks we are aware of but don't understand— governments might know that pandemic diseases in general are a risk they can plan for, for example, but they can't know the exact nature of what new disease might arise next. In computing, this might be the next big virus or a new kind of security breach. When hardware is fixed and software is monolithic, we have a very good grasp of the known unknowns. But with complex systems, this is not the case.

Unknown knowns

"Unknown knowns" are the risks you aren't aware of but can understand: biases, intuitions, and unconscious decisions are good examples. You might know in a general sense that all companies have vulnerabilities, yet miss those within your own department. In tech, this could look like a rogue employee or team making unapproved decisions that end up having disastrous consequences.

Unknown unknowns

Finally, the "unknown unknowns" are the hardest to prepare for: the risks that you aren't even thinking about, the ones that come completely out of left field, which you neither anticipate nor understand. Alien spaceships showing up to attack Earth, like in the movie *Independence Day*, would be an unknown unknown. In the cloud, this might be more like the cascading supply-chain disruptions caused by Covid-19. When hardware is immutable and elastic and software is distributed, there is a greater potential to encounter new unknown unknowns. Traditional monitoring tools aren't much help with this kind of risk.

That's why many companies are embracing new ways of monitoring in the cloud. Here I'll look at four of the most important of these: observability, testing in production, chaos engineering, and AIOps.

OBSERVABILITY

The term *observability* stems from *control theory*, which is the idea that two control systems—inner controls and outer controls—work against our tendencies to deviate. *Observability* is a measure of how well the internal states of a system can be inferred from knowledge of its external outputs. To put it another way, if you can observe the outside of a system to determine what is going on inside it, you have observability.

I'll illustrate with an example of how a company embarked on an important digital initiative and ran into reliability issues after launch due to an unknown unknown: Covid-19.

A company I'll call Scrumptious has been a top brand in the food industry for decades, with great revenue growth. It did not feel the need to jump on the bandwagon and embrace a digital strategy. Then the Covid-19 pandemic hit.

Suddenly, brands that had implemented a digital strategy over the years were better able to engage with their customers than companies like Scrumptious were. Those brands could provide real-time offers and deals, and were able to implement curb, pickup, and home delivery strategies within a few weeks.

To catch up to its competitors, Scrumptious hired a digital agency to create a new .com website for the brand. The new look had all the new bells and whistles one would expect from a modern web page and mobile app. All of the customer feedback sessions were extremely positive, and initial pilot testing went smoothly. The new website refresh was going to be a hit. A few trade magazines wrote articles about the new website, and the CEO did interviews on TV. The media attention drove an unprecedented amount of traffic, but the operations team anticipated this, and their years of experience served them well. Team members celebrated as the wall of monitors showed nothing but green statuses and health checks.

But then the phones started ringing. The brand name Scrumptious started trending on Twitter—in a negative light. How could this be? Everything was green. Soon the team realized that a few features of the website were performing slowly and occasionally timing out. Customers were struggling to place orders for home delivery. For the next 24 hours the team scrambled to pinpoint the problem. They worked through the night to fix it. Eventually all services were restored and the website was back to performing as expected. The problem, as it turned out, was that two of the external APIs were being overwhelmed with traffic and responding slowly—but only in a few geographies. The APIs were all returning a successful return code, so the monitoring systems showed that everything was green.

Scrumptious had been very proud of the reliability of its old website. Over the years, the operations team had perfected the art of maintaining it, and customers were accustomed to fast performance. Now the team was suddenly dealing with a new cloud-based website built by an external vendor, which was calling multiple APIs from other external vendors (food delivery companies like Door-Dash, for instance). This complex architecture introduced numerous unknown unknowns, yet the ops team was only equipped with the old tools and processes that had served them well when all they were concerned with were known knowns.

What could the Scrumptious teams have done differently? From their monitoring, everything looked healthy. Eventually, the system's performance started degrading as the API responses queued up, but the customer was already feeling the impact. What questions could they have asked their monitoring solutions? They could only ask questions based on the metrics they had chosen to monitor. Geography wasn't something they were monitoring, so they had no way to know that only certain geographies were being affected. All they were monitoring was the API call. How could they have supplemented their monitoring solutions with more data? Through instrumentation.

Instrumentation means writing code inside a system that creates necessary metrics, timestamps, statuses, or other relevant data that can be used to observe that system. Monitoring metrics are an aggregation of data. For example, the metric *throughput* is an average over a period of time. Instrumentation allows you to add more detailed data and store it in its raw form in an observability platform or some other source, so you can query it and ask more specific questions, like "Where is the throughput degrading?" or "What path did the service take?" By instrumenting your code, you can leave a trail of breadcrumbs in the logs to help you better troubleshoot the unknown unknowns.

TESTING IN PRODUCTION

Traditionally, testing requires an environment for each stage of the development life cycle. Developers develop on their laptops or in a dedicated development environment. Code is merged, built, and deployed in a testing environment. When the code is deemed ready for some final testing, it's deployed to a staging environment before deployment to production.

The staging environment is configured to be very close to the configuration environment, but often does not have as much memory, CPU, disks, and nodes as the actual production environment because of the costs. In addition, developers and testers are not allowed to see or use sensitive data, such as personally identifiable information and protected healthcare data. Such data is either totally excluded from the system or masked, so that the attributes containing sensitive data cannot be seen. This means that staging is not an exact match for the production environment—which, if you think about it, defeats the purpose of having a staging environment. Staging provides a certain degree of comfort: you can learn that the code has a good chance of working as expected in production, but you won't know for *sure* until after it is deployed.

With complex systems, any difference in infrastructure, data, configuration, and end user interaction between staging and production will almost guarantee that the deployment will encounter some unexpected results. All you can do is hope that none of them are catastrophic.

To mitigate this risk, testers and reliability engineers run tests in production to get a better sense of how well the new code works once it is deployed. To many people, especially those in risk and security, this is outrageous: how can we let anyone test *in production?* They imagine a QA person running scripts in a production environment with unproven code. In reality, testing in production is an *additional* testing process that advances the quality of software after deployment, while reducing the blast radius of any problems that arise when new code is released.

But this isn't really anything new. To illustrate, let's take an example that will be familiar to anyone who has worked in retail: pilot stores.

Early in my career, I worked with a retailer I'll call FoodShop that had a thousand grocery stores. The company decided to deploy a new software release to its store system that would run locally at each store. Deploying this code to all of the thousand stores at once would have been risky: if the software took down the point of sale system, nobody would be able to check out and revenue would be lost on a large scale.

To mitigate this risk, FoodShop instead deployed the new release to a group of stores called *pilot stores*, usually between 5 and 10 stores, that served as an experimental group. They monitored the stores for a week or two and if everything seemed stable, they pushed the code to the next set of stores, maybe 25 to 50. They continued this process until the software had been successfully deployed in enough stores to convince FoodShop that the risk was low. Only then did they deploy to the rest of their stores. Retailers have been doing this for decades. This is testing in production.

Testing in production in cloud-based systems involves some similar strategies. Let's compare and contrast six of the most popular.

The big bang method

"Big bang" deployments were a popular method back when we deployed monoliths a few times a year and shipped software to customers. As we moved to online systems that are "always on," we no longer had the luxury of scheduling downtime to update software. Yet many companies still leverage this model, which requires extensive testing windows to reduce the risk of the defects when the previous version is replaced with a new version.

In this method, you perform your last quality checks in a staging environment, which—as I highlighted above—is most likely *not* a very accurate replica of production. Then you deploy the code and hope you've caught enough defects in the staging environment. It often takes an outage to do this type of deployment; if you need to roll back, another outage will be required. In the age of online systems, latency is often perceived as downtime, so planned outages for deployments are mostly unacceptable. We must look for better approaches.

Rolling updates

One better approach is rolling updates. With rolling updates, you deploy new software to a subset of your infrastructure and monitor the results in production. This is the software equivalent of the pilot-store method. This model works when the infrastructure is both distributed and dedicated to a group of users. In the retail example, each store has its own dedicated system that operates entirely separately from the others; here, you have infrastructure for a specific group of users that runs separately from everything else.

As you test the software and your deployments stabilize, you deploy to more servers and repeat the process (shown in Figure 7-3). Eventually all systems get the new software. This is much less risky than the all-or-nothing "big bang" approach, and it limits the impact of any incidents to a subset of the user base.

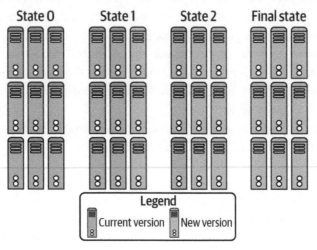

Figure 7-3. Rolling updates

Blue/green deployments

Blue/green deployments take the rolling approach a step further. First, you put a load balancer in front of the infrastructure. Then you deploy a new instance of the production environment, referred to as the "green" environment, while the current production environment is "blue." You perform tests on the green environment while production continues as usual in the original (blue) environment.

Once testing is complete and you obtain approval to deploy, you configure the load balancer to point to the green environment. If there are issues in the new green environment that create the need to roll back, you simply change the load balancer to point back to the blue environment (Figure 7-4) until you are ready to try again in the green environment.

The advantage here is that the rollback process is much simpler and less risky than the old way, where you had to roll back software from a production environment. In this model you never change the current production infrastructure; in the old model you had to update production, then carefully undo those updates when rolling back. Another advantage is that you are testing in an identical production environment with real production data and traffic, unlike the staging environment, so your tests are much more likely to reflect what will happen in real life.

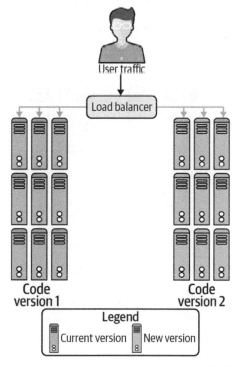

Figure 7-4. Blue/green testing: testing in the green environment, deploying to the blue environment

Canary deployments

Canary deployments reduce the amount of risk exposure of deployments even further. Like blue/green deployments, canary deployments leverage an exact copy of the production environment to push the new code to and test in. The difference here is that with canary releases, you can direct a subset of users to the new environments and test in *parallel* with the production systems (Figure 7-5). If anything goes wrong, you simply stop sending transactions from the test group to the new environment and direct them back to the existing production environment. If testing in the new environment is successful, you can either fully switch over to the new environment or direct another group of users to the new production environment.

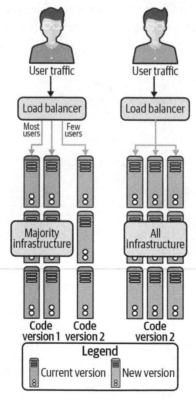

Figure 7-5. Canary deployments

This method combines rollout updates and blue/green deployments, so that you can validate software in the actual production environment and gradually upgrade it over time as you become comfortable that it's working as planned.

Testing in production methods like rolling updates, blue/green deployments, and canary releases are actually improved methods of practices developers have been using for decades. These methods are in fact much easier to implement in cloud-based systems, since we are not dealing with physical infrastructure. Making copies of cloud infrastructure is a coding exercise, whereas making copies of physical infrastructure is both expensive and time-consuming.

Chaos engineering

Companies that are very advanced at testing in production often take the concept to the next level: chaos engineering. Chaos engineering is a disciplined, proactive approach to identifying failures and potential breaking points in a system before they become outages. If done right, chaos engineering can increase reliability, reduce unplanned work and toil, help you avoid downtime, and help you prepare for incidents and outages.

Chaos engineering is a key strategy for high-scale distributed systems. In the book *Chaos Engineering* (O'Reilly), Casey Rosenthal and Nora Jones describe their method for performing chaos experiments:

1. Start by defining "steady state" as some measurable output of a system that indicates normal behavior.

2. Hypothesize that this steady state will continue in both the control group and the experimental group.

3. Introduce variables that reflect real-world events, like servers that crash, hard drives that malfunction, network connections that are severed, etc.

4. Try to disprove the hypothesis by looking for a difference in steady state between the control group and the experimental group.

Netflix is famous for creating the Simian Army, a collection of tools for deliberately causing failures within a system. Netflix engineers watch those failures carefully and learn from them, so they can design the system to auto-heal or compensate for outages with minimal impact to the users.

Many people think chaos engineering is "breaking things in production," which is why many companies refrain from adopting it. A better way to think about chaos engineering is "fixing things in production." Chaos experiments don't necessarily have to break things by stopping infrastructure components: they can also alter load, introduce latency, create standards violations, or introduce abnormalities to the system in other ways. The idea caught on, and over the last several years, several vendors have built chaos engineering platforms to assist with chaos experiments.

But before you attempt to leverage chaos engineering in your system, there are some prerequisites. The target applications should already have failure capabilities, automated tests, and a mature CI/CD pipeline. The team conducting the experiments should already have modern monitoring solutions in place and be well versed in concepts such as observability. To quote Charity Majors, cofounder and CTO of the observability platform Honeycomb.io, "Without observability, you don't have chaos engineering. You just have chaos."[3]

Let's take a hypothetical example so you can see chaos engineering in action. FestiveCorp is expecting a seasonal spike in traffic as the winter holidays approach. To prepare, the team wants to run some experiments to ensure that the systems can withstand the expected increase.

First they define the key metrics of the system in its normal, daily steady state. Then they create a hypothesis: "Under demand at five times the normal volume of requests, we expect that the system will maintain its steady state."

Next, they introduce conditions into the system, such as increases in request volume and latency. They shut down web servers to use an approach similar to the canary deployment method, where only a control group is affected by the experiments.

When the FestiveCorp team runs the experiments, they discover that, from an infrastructure standpoint, the system performs admirably, thanks to some recent enhancements in autoscaling. However, some transactions are being lost during server shutdowns. They recognize this as an opportunity to improve, and decide to leverage a queueing system to guarantee delivery of each request.

Performing these types of experiments in production can give management heartburn. I highly recommend starting your chaos engineering journey in nonproduction environments until your staff's skills and tooling become mature enough to run experiments in production. Discovering issues in nonproduction environments can be beneficial for fixing system weakness before going to production, but when you do, remember that you are only validating the system's

---

3 Charity Majors, presentation at Chaos Community Day (https://www.slideshare.net/CharityMajors/chaos-engineering-without-observability-is-just-chaos), New York, 2019.

steady state for the environment you are experimenting in, not the production environment.

Synthetic testing

Synthetic testing is the practice of running simulated users, or bots, in the production system to exercise certain features that test performance and availability. It's been around for a while, but is gaining popularity amid the complexity of distributed systems.

Let's go back to FoodShop, the grocery chain. We built a digital coupon website where consumers could select offers for their local grocery store. These offers would go into the shopper's digital wallet (stored in the cloud), to be redeemed at any FoodShop location. My company white-labeled our website so that it appeared to be part of the retailer's main brand page. The appearance and performance of our webpage was critical to the brand's reputation.

On the backend, we had plenty of monitoring solutions to ensure that all the components were available and performing according to their SLOs. We monitored the infrastructure, database, network, web traffic, security controls, and more. The developers had access to an application performance monitoring tool so they could set alerts to track trends in performance. We pinged all of the APIs every few minutes to make sure they were still working. We felt pretty good about our setup.

Then, one day, an angry retailer called us to inform us that their help desk was getting overwhelmed with failed login errors. We looked at our monitoring solutions and everything looked healthy—all the dashboards were green. After performing an analysis, we found that the authentication API was not executing, even though it showed as available when we pinged it. Since the API never executed, we saw no failures or performance degradation in our monitoring solutions—nothing out of the ordinary.

The retailer asked us, "Don't you monitor your systems?" My heart sank. If they only knew the investments we'd made in time and resources to make this product reliable! The fix was easy: we simply restarted the authentication service. But the problem was that our customers' customers found out about the outage before we did. That can't happen.

To make sure this scenario never happened again, we adopted synthetic testing. We created a fictitious retailer account and fictitious retail customers. We then automated jobs that continuously simulated users exercising every single API call within our system. This allowed us to monitor the performance and health of each API and ensure that the use case of a pingable API that was not executing would never catch us off guard again.

Synthetic testing can be used in conjunction with all of the methods described above. It is very useful for testing and monitoring systems in complex environments where infrastructure expands and contracts on demand.

Monitoring and AIOps

In this chapter, I have discussed numerous ways to test, deploy, and run experiments to improve the reliability of complex systems in the cloud. But there's more: you also have to step up your monitoring game. To do that, you'll need intelligent monitoring.

Distributed cloud-based systems are becoming so complex that it's impossible for human beings to monitor everything going on within them. That's why companies are starting to embrace AIOps, the practice of using artificial intelligence (AI) and machine learning (ML) in systems to help monitor complexity. Let's take a moment to clarify our terms:

Artificial intelligence (AI)
This is a broad term, but the authors of *The AI Ladder* define it as technology that "makes it possible for machines to learn from experience, adjust to new inputs, and perform human-like tasks through the combination of math and computer science."[4]

Intelligent operations (AIOps)
Gartner (*https://blogs.gartner.com/andrew-lerner/2017/08/09/aiops-platforms*) offers the following definition:

AIOps platforms utilize big data, modern machine learning and other advanced analytics technologies to directly and indirectly enhance IT operations (monitoring, automation and service desk) functions with proactive, personal, and dynamic insight. AIOps platforms enable the concurrent use of multiple data sources, data collection methods, analytical (real-time and deep) technologies, and presentation technologies.

Machine learning (ML)
Machine learning is the algorithmic ability of a machine or computer system to learn from data and use it to predict outcomes.

---

4 Rob Thomas and Paul Zikopolous, *The AI Ladder* (O'Reilly), Chapter 2.

While these terms get thrown around a lot, you need to understand that there's actually a broad spectrum of monitoring operations. Reactive and proactive operations are entirely done by humans, while AIOps methods vary in how heavily they utilize AI (as shown in Figure 7-6). Your organization will most likely adopt a method somewhere between the extremes. Let's walk through them one by one, starting with the most human-centered approach, reactive operations.

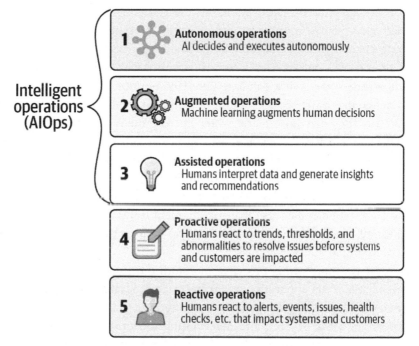

Figure 7-6. Monitoring systems that use AI are part of a spectrum of monitoring possibilities with varying degrees of reliability and advance notice

Reactive operations

Reactive operations is the term used to describe reacting to alerts and events only when caused by system issues, such as "server is down" or "storage device is out of space." In the reactive approach to operations, you monitor infrastructure and application components, and raise alerts when a component begins failing or a key metric exceeds an allowable threshold.

There are several problems with this approach. First, if a component fails, it is likely to cause a cascade of other problems. Second, when a system gets to this point, the likelihood of customers experiencing an outage or degraded reliability is high. Third, this type of monitoring does not take a broader look at the overall system; it focuses only on specific components. This type of monitoring is necessary, but it is not enough for systems that are "always on."

Proactive operations

Proactive monitoring solutions are still human-based, but take a more holistic approach. As proactive monitoring tools monitor the overall system, they create historical averages of the performance of the components of the system. The tools also allow you to monitor "units of work," or transactions. For example, when a new user registers to become a customer, the process involves a combination of several backend services interfacing with a web tier, a caching tier, an application server tier, and a database tier. The monitoring tools can be configured to define that entire flow as a unit of work and establish its average performance. Then they can raise alerts when the key metrics start to trend a few percentage points below the average.

These proactive alerts allow operations and developers to discover and fix problems before users ever become aware of them (hopefully). This type of monitoring can help you discover issues like an underperforming Apache server that needs to be restarted, a database that could benefit from adding more threads, or an opportunity to increase cache levels to get data from memory more often instead of having to query from disk.

Like reactive monitoring, proactive monitoring includes monitoring individual components of the application and infrastructure stacks—but it also provides a wider view of the system. But proactive monitoring is still not enough. Creating the appropriate units of work and determining the proper metrics to monitor comes from experience learned from prior or anticipated events. AI can take monitoring to the next level.

Intelligent operations

Intelligent operations leverages AI and machine learning so that the system can alert us of the unknowns.

There are three levels of Intelligent operations:

Assisted operations
> *Assisted operations* uses artificial intelligence to detect patterns or trends and then generates insights or recommendations, which humans interpret as they decide whether they want to take action or not.

A business use case for assisted operations is fraud detection: when you travel, your purchases may trigger a fraud alert from your credit card company. You'll get a text to let you know that the system has detected abnormal activity on your account. The process does not take any further action until you respond that you made the purchase or that you think the transaction may be fraudulent.

This same approach can be used for anomaly and threat detection on cloud systems. The amount of data in the logs of an enterprise cloud platform is just way too much for a human to consume, let alone provide any valuable insights on. AI can analyze the data and traffic patterns, and recognize patterns that mimic suspicious behaviors, like botnets, malicious scripts, and denial of service attacks, and alert the appropriate people to take action.

Augmented operations

Augmented operations monitoring goes one step further by remediating the problem immediately on its own. It then alerts the appropriate people of the action it has taken. For example, if the AI detects malicious intent on an instance, it can choose to take that instance offline immediately. This swift action, known as autoremediation, can prevent further harm from incurring on the instance, with no human intervention.

Autonomous operations

In *autonomous operations*, the AI discovers the insights and acts automatically, like augmented operations does; the difference is that the process completes *without human intervention*.

Self-driving cars are a good example of autonomous systems. Edge computing, too, provides numerous use cases. *Edge computing* describes systems where the code runs on devices and systems that live neither in datacenters nor in clouds. Instead, these systems live where the producers and consumers of data and events are: inside the devices we use every day. Engineers, operations, and everyone else working in tech now need to manage large numbers of sensors and IP-enabled devices out in the world. It is not feasible to send people to repair or restart thousands of devices and beacons, from tractors in cornfields to motion sensors on airplanes to robotic vacuums in living rooms. These use cases are driving the demand for more fully autonomous operations capabilities.

In summary, there are several modern approaches to dealing with unexpected outcomes. We discussed observability, testing in production, canary and blue green releases, chaos engineering, and AIOps. Most companies I visit are using very few if any of these methods. Cloud architectures can be quite complex to manage due to being distributed and elastic. As more workloads move to the cloud, the ability of humans to manage all of the infrastructure and applications becomes extremely challenging using the methods we used in the datacenter. We need automation, intelligence, and the ability to test systems in their actual environments to make some of the unknowns known, so we can improve the reliability of systems.

Conclusion

You may be overwhelmed by the number of new approaches to operations that I've introduced in this chapter. All require some level of maturity in both operations and cloud computing. You might not start your cloud journey by embracing all of these concepts, and that's fine. In order to scale and grow from ten to a hundred to a thousand applications in the cloud, though, you will need to start adopting some of the operations techniques you've just read about.

As more workloads start running on the cloud, scaling operations has to mean more than just hiring more people. It needs to mean a combination of staffing, automation, leveraging AI, and proactively improving reliability to reduce toil. Each one of these concepts requires a change of mindset, away from the old ways of testing and operating systems.

As the DevOps guru and Tripwire founder Gene Kim told me on one of my podcasts (*https://oreil.ly/qUVAC*) recently, "There has never been a better time to be in infrastructure." I would add that there has never been a better time to be in ops. Ops has a huge role to play in the overall reliability of cloud applications. If you take anything away from this chapter, understand that reliability can make all the difference in accelerating or stifling cloud adoption in an enterprise.

8

Conclusion: Moving Forward, Embracing Change

When I first started my cloud journey in 2008, the public cloud was used primarily for infrastructure services for compute, network, and storage. By 2010, the CSPs were offering fully managed services for databases that auto-provisioned, managed, and scaled all of the necessary infrastructure and database software for you. Then came containers, functions as a service (FaaS), data streaming and ingestion services, and more abstractions of specific technology components. Next, the providers started abstracting entire technology stacks for specific use cases like Internet of Things (IoT), blockchain, and gaming. As I write this in 2020, the CSPs are abstracting entire business functions. Google's Healthcare API, for example, is designed to ingest healthcare data and images in industry-specific standard formats, complete with de-identification logic for masking personal data.

The difference is striking. Think about the recommendations Amazon offers customers: based on what you've bought and what it knows about you, the site recommends new purchases, often with incredible accuracy. Back in the 1990s, I had a team of developers who worked on building code that would produce similar recommendations. We wrote hundreds of thousands of lines of code, which ran on massive infrastructure that needed to be maintained. Today, Amazon offers its purchase-behavior recommendation logic as an API. I could replace all of that code, infrastructure, and operations with simple API calls.

The innovations keep coming, and each one offers another layer of abstraction—giving enterprises the opportunity to offload the heavy lifting of building and managing the underlying infrastructure and algorithms. Instead, you can leverage a fully managed service and vastly improve much greater speed to market if you take advantage of it in a thoughtful and forward-thinking way. Each innovation is a challenge to engineers and architects, asking us to rethink how we build and operate software.

As we offload ever more work to the CSPs, enterprises must continuously reevaluate their architecture, best practices, business processes, and operating models. Embracing change, not resisting it, is the way forward.

Organizational Change Management as a Practice

Organizational and culture change can be very hard to implement. Change of any kind can disrupt the flow of business, create new risks, introduce talent gaps, and cause political stress, among many other issues. That's why so many decision-makers resist it! But remember this: the longer it takes a company to embrace a change or a shift in mindset, the harder and more expensive it will be to implement that change. What's more, new technologies like cloud, AI, chaos engineering, etc. are all challenging us to rethink how we do our jobs. The problem is that we are addressing change in silos, creating conflicting strategies and operating models. We need a more holistic view of the impacts of change to the enterprise.

Yet the answer isn't as simple as "all the change, everywhere, immediately." When deploying software to the cloud for the first time, as you learned in Chapter 7, you don't take a "big bang" approach. You usually select a small number of applications and build the minimal viable cloud: the minimum set of controls and policies based on the requirements of those applications.

The same goes for culture and organizational change. It's best to start with only as much transformation as you need to implement the first step of the change. If you're only moving two applications into the cloud, you might not need to establish a governing body, like the CCOP discussed in Chapter 5. But when you get to one hundred applications, you'd better have some form of governance in place.

Similarly, if your initial venture into the cloud only involves a couple of small teams, you probably don't yet need to redesign your HR incentives for cloud engineers or establish a massive plan to reskill thousands of IT professionals. You might only need to tweak a few legacy processes.

But as you bring more applications to the cloud, you must start transforming your organization toward a new operating model geared to delivering products and services in the cloud. Investing in change management is a critical success factor for any large cloud transformation.

There are numerous methodologies for driving large-scale change. You don't have to—and shouldn't try to—create your own. While evaluating them all is outside the scope of this book, I strongly recommend that you research change-management frameworks, pick one, and run with it.

The two methodologies I prefer are John Kotter's eight-step change model[1] and the Lean Transformation Framework (*https://www.lean.org/WhatsLean/Trans formationFramework.cfm*). In both models, the first step is identifying your "why." Kotter frames the "why" in the context of a compelling event: what is driving the change, and why is it important to the business and the individuals within it? Whether you pick one of these frameworks or a different one, the "why" is incredibly important. If there isn't a compelling reason for change, it is extremely difficult to get people to think and act differently. It is much easier to do what you know and are comfortable with. If there is a compelling event with specific messaging, people will be more apt to align with the journey. That messaging might be something like:

1. We need to consolidate from 10 datacenters to 2 in the next 24 months by leveraging the public cloud.

2. We need to empower our data scientists with a cloud-based data analytics platform by quarter four to leapfrog our competition.

3. We are going to become a digital bank and disrupt our industry.

I urge you to strongly consider formalizing organizational change management as a key business function, even up to creating an Office of Change. Dedicating people to organizational and cultural change allows a company to take a pragmatic approach to change, led by people who are skilled change agents. They will know how to plan communications, build training programs, work with HR to rethink goals and objectives to drive new behaviors, and even perform value-stream mapping workshops to remove bottlenecks from business processes. Most importantly, the professionals in your Office of Change will focus on designing and implementing these processes as their core responsibility, rather than attempting to do it when and where they can while performing another key function.

---

1 See John P. Kotter, *Leading Change* (Harvard Business Review Press), and *Accelerate* (Harvard Business Review Press).

I often get pushback from IT leaders about organizational change management: they laughingly refer to it as "the soft stuff." These same leaders also ask me why they are still struggling to get anyone on board with cloud adoption after two or three years of trying to implement it. Well, the soft stuff is a critical part of accelerating cloud adoption. Pay attention to it, get to know it, and invest in it.

Looking Ahead: What to Expect

In today's environment, speed to market is the new currency. Companies that can react quickly to address new or changing market demands will win. If you don't keep up with the pace of change, you risk standing by as your products and services are replaced by those of companies that are leveraging newer technologies and getting to market faster. As I look into my crystal ball to predict the next five years, I see the pace of change accelerating even faster. Here is how I see the next few years playing out. I encourage you to research these trends yourself and see if you agree.

MORE ABSTRACTIONS

Here is a pattern that I have seen over and over in my 35 years in IT:

- A new technology or concept emerges.
- Practitioners spend a few years perfecting its implementation.
- The solution becomes commoditized.
- The solution is abstracted to gain efficiency and speed to market.

This pattern has played out in software development languages, for instance. We went from machine code and Assembler to third-generation languages like COBOL and C, and fourth-generation languages like Python, Ruby, and PHP, all the way to the low-code/no-code solutions emerging today. Each generation of languages further abstracts the underlying instructions of the previous generation, the need for developers to focus on low-level programming tasks like calling a register in assembly, creating a doubly linked list in Fortran, or performing garbage collection in Java. Are these examples unfamiliar to you? That's because they have been abstracted in the languages that you use.

The abstractions I see happening in the cloud are profound. We already have abstractions in the form of cloud service models: IaaS, PaaS, and SaaS. I believe that the 2020s will see widespread adoption of serverless computing, where developers leverage both fully managed services and functions as a service (FaaS) as the predominant way to build applications. At the same time, CSPs will build more business functions as services.

I also expect a boom in industry-specific APIs as certain business functions become commoditized. Building applications and services will become increasingly fast.

MORE EDGE COMPUTING

Edge computing, which I touched on briefly in Chapter 7, is a paradigm where processing is performed directly on devices or sensors, or on infrastructure located close to those devices or sensors—*not* within a datacenter or cloud. Almost everything that can be equipped with a sensor will be equipped with a sensor. I've spent an entire book discussing the differences between building software for datacenters versus for clouds, and it would take another book to discuss the differences between cloud and edge computing.[2] And you guessed it, we will see hybrid architectures that span cloud and edge, datacenter and edge, and all three.

THE DEATH OF THE KEYBOARD

Every year, fewer and fewer people do their computing on a keyboard. In 2013, mobile usage made up 16.2% of all internet traffic, and in 2016, mobile internet usage surpassed computer usage for the first time. Between 2013 and 2020, mobile usage has gone up 222%. It now accounts for more than 53% of all internet traffic. That doesn't even count tablets and other small nonphone devices.[3] The user interfaces of the future will be driven by voice and image recognition. This means that our applications must be more adaptive and must account for unreliable connectivity.

THE CONTINUED RISE OF AI AND MACHINE LEARNING

Training machine learning models used to take weeks to months and required a significant investment in infrastructure and highly skilled data scientists. Much of this work is now being commoditized and abstracted as services that are fully managed by CSPs, and this acceleration of AI- and ML-based application delivery is likely to continue.

---

2 Some good places to start are Chapter 19 of Lee Atchison, *Architecting for Scale*, 2nd ed. (O'Reilly), and Dominik Ryzko's *Modern Big Data Architectures* (Wiley).

3 Broadband Search, "Mobile vs. Desktop Internet Usage (Latest 2020 Data)" (*https://www.broadband search.net/blog/mobile-desktop-internet-usage-statistics*).

As discussed in the section on AIOps in Chapter 7, artificial intelligence and machine learning can be leveraged to provide assisted, augmented, or autonomous business processes. The use of these technologies can disrupt industries. Urban planners (*https://oreil.ly/hIwHL*) are implementing cloud and edge technologies in conjunction with AI and ML technologies to create smart cities that reduce traffic, optimize trash pickup, predict weather events, and much more.

AI and ML can also help brands personalize their digital engagement strategies. By putting together datasets ranging from purchase data to social data, these systems provide insights that companies can use to better serve customers. These technologies are already in wide use, but expect their reach and accuracy to continue growing.

NEW COMPETITORS THAT DON'T EXIST YET

Back in the day of packaged software, once a customer bought and installed the package software for a large fee and a 20% annual maintenance fee, they were locked in for a long time. Now we are entering a subscription model where companies can pay for services instead of large monolithic software products. Products are now being built as a collection of services. If a top competitor or startup emerges that can provide that service better with more modern capabilities, the customer can unsubscribe to that particular service and get it from the other vendors.

Some large companies focus so much on their known competitors that they don't pay enough attention to emerging startups. Startups are not mired in legacy and bureaucracy, and have the ability to build from a clean slate. They are leveraging all of the power of the cloud and can move at lightning speed. Just look at how Airbnb took market share away from the hotel industry, and Uber disrupted the taxi and limousine companies. You can't know what future competitors will disrupt your industry; plan accordingly. Large corporations will always be slower than small companies and startups, but they can still be agile enough to fend off the competition. Companies should put as much weight into improving agility as they do toward securing the cloud. Remember, agility is a competitive advantage.

Future-Proofing Your Cloud Adoption

A flurry of rapid change is coming your way in the next few years. While you are ramping up your team to embrace one set of technologies, another set of technology opportunities will present itself. The strategies I've presented in this book for transforming your people, processes, and technologies will remain relevant as the cloud changes and as future technologies continue to evolve. Just as the VP of Electricity you met at the beginning of this book couldn't have imagined cloud computing, we can't imagine what innovations are yet to come, but we know that they will come, and we need to be ready.

That's why it's so important to embrace a mindset that expects and is ready for constant change. The old ways of doing things served businesses well for decades, but they won't serve well in the future. Your journey into the cloud is just the beginning: once you're there, you'll unlock future technologies and innovations you haven't even dreamed of yet. To take full advantage of them, you must redesign your business processes, corporate culture, and operating models for the cloud—and for what comes after the cloud. Put the customer and the product at the center of everything you do—and never stop learning.

Index

About the Author

Mike Kavis has served in numerous technical roles such as CTO, chief architect, and VP positions with more than 30 years of experience in software development and architecture. A pioneer in cloud computing, Kavis led a team that built the world's first high-speed transaction network in Amazon's public cloud and won the 2010 AWS Global Startup Challenge. Kavis is the author of *Architecting the Cloud: Design Decisions for Cloud Computing Service Models*(Wiley, 2014).

Colophon

The illustration on the cover of *Accelerating Cloud Adoption* was designed by Randy Comer.

The cover fonts are Gilroy and Guardian Sans Condensed. The text font is Scala Pro and the heading font is Benton Sans.

Lightning Source UK Ltd.
Milton Keynes UK
UKHW020145060121
376481UK00008B/20